CHICAGO PUBLIC LIBRARY
WOODSON REGIONAL
9525 S. HALSTED ST.  60628

# *BYLINE:*
## *Guide*
## *rea*

**THE CHICAGO PUBLIC LIBRARY**

CHICAGO PUBLIC LIBRARY
WOODSON REGIONAL
9525 S. HALSTED ST.  60628

**FORM 19**

# BYLINE

## *AN INSIDER'S GUIDE TO CHICAGO-AREA PRINT MEDIA*

National Writers Union, Chicago Local 12
© 1994 by the National Writers Union
All rights reserved. Published 1994
Printed in the United States of America

ISBN 0-9637796-0-5

# Table of Contents

Foreward by Bill Granger

## BY THE WAY

| | |
|---|---|
| Publish or Perish? by Kathy S. Wilson | 7 |
| Salt on the Wound by S.L. Wisenberg | 11 |
| The New Covenant by Ron Dorfman | 14 |
| It's Your Problem by Betty Sherwood | 17 |
| Going to Small Claims Court by Keith Watson | 23 |
| Two Views on Public Releations | |
|    Working with Public Relations by Len Strazewski | 29 |
|    Publicists are Writers' Allies by Michele Kelly | 32 |
| Trading on Your Adaptability by Jerry DeMuth | 35 |

## BY PUBLICATION

| | |
|---|---|
| Publications Listings | 41 |
| Kill Fees Listings | 131 |
| Payment Policies Listings | 132 |
| Contract Types Listings | 133 |

## BY THE BOOK

| | |
|---|---|
| Special Libraries in the Chicago Area by LeVaughn Jones | 137 |

## BY WRITERS

| | |
|---|---|
| Introduction by Keith Watson | 157 |
| Advertising Age by Anne Aldrich | 159 |
| Chicago Magazine by Michael O'Neill | 161 |
| Chicago Reader by Sheila Malkind | 163 |
| Chicago Sun-Times by Aaron Cohen | 164 |
| Chicago Tribune by Kurt Jacobsen | 166 |
| Crain's Chicago Business by Marilyn Soltis | 168 |
| In These Times by Steve Askin | 170 |

## BY THE BACK

| | |
|---|---|
| A Better Contract | 175 |
| Byline Contributors | 177 |
| Writer's Bloc | 180 |

# Foreward

## Writers Talk About Their Business, Not Their Art

*By Bill Granger*

Non-writers are under the impression that when writers get together, they talk about their art.

This impression is fostered in numerous literary biographies in which Charles Dickens is palling around with Wilkes Collins or James Boswell is eating and drinking with Samuel Johnson.

According to the biographies, when great writers got together, it was to talk about art.

These impressions are wrong, of course. Doubtless, art worms its way into conversations between writers. But if there is too much posturing and bragging involved, one of the writers will soon grow bored and end the art-strewn conversation.

What writers really talk about is the business.

Dickens and Collins talked about money. Boswell and Johnson talked about money. They talked about how much they got for a piece and who was offering more. They talked about crap editors and crap agents and the whole crappy business. And every now and then, to break the tension or tedium of it all, as Ernest Hemingway recounted in *A Moveable Feast*, his best book about writers, they talked about food, drink, sex, or maybe even art.

Writers are alone in a lonely trade, and they have no idea of what they are worth or what their work is worth.

For that reason alone, it seems, the National Writers Union is going against the grain of reality. Unionized freelance writers is an oxymoron.

On the other hand, just by beginning to exchange information, the union is treading on ancient turf. Writers have always compared notes on the business with each other. Why not do more than that? Why not compare notes, share information about the way of contracts and editors and the world of letters in an honest way? Of course, some writers will write for nothing just to see the glory of their name in print. They undermine the trade of those who write for a living. Other writers will lie for the sake of currying favor with some editor or publication. Both groups should be boiled in ink.

But most writers are just trying to figure out the changing nature of the game. I think the union is a good idea because it is a start at making some sense of the rules. Like, why do some agents charge 10 percent and most charge 15 percent? And when does holding books as reserve against returns become holding books hostage? Why do some magazines pay kill fees and why do some magazines pay on publication? Because, partly, it's the same old "the squeeky wheel gets greased," and everyone is still waiting for the Streeterville bus. It's a matter that freelance writers don't want to face: they are disorganized and weak.

I joined the union to get health-care coverage. That was in October 1992. I talked it over with Jerry DeMuth, a fellow freelance writer and former newspaper colleague. It sounded like a good, somewhat quixotic organization. And besides, it offered health care. Four months later, my wife got a job with excellent fringe benefits, including total health care, and I dropped my health-care coverage with the union.

I did not drop out of the union. Come October again, I will sign up for another year and send in my dues. I tell every freelance writer I know about the union. Like I said—or tried to say—I don't quite know where the union is heading, but the ride should be interesting. Don't you think Hemingway and Dickens would have joined as well?

# By THE WAY

## Succeeding at the Writing Life

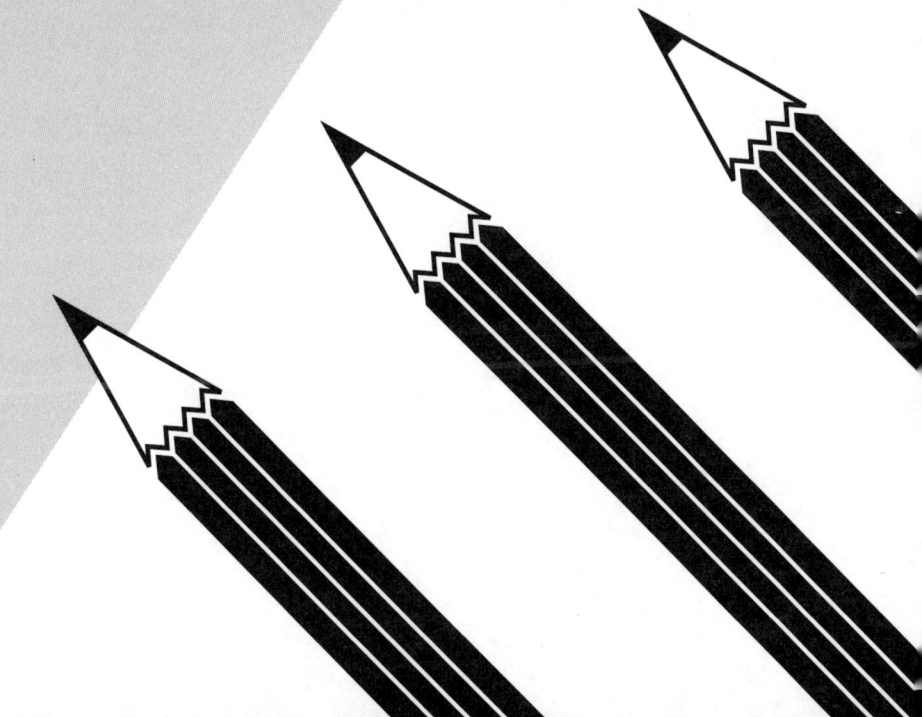

# Publish or Perish?

## Tips on Getting Bylines in Chicago

*By Kathy S. Wilson*

Editors from the *Chicago Reader*, the *Chicago Tribune*, *Crain's Chicago Business*, and *Chicago* magazine attended a freelance writers forum sponsored by the Chicago local of the National Writers Union and provided invaluable tips for journalists on how to maximize their chances of getting published. Their unifying advice: Study and understand a publication and its market niche before sending the editor a strongly focused query letter.

*The Reader* is a free, alternative weekly in four sections. Each issue includes at least one in-depth feature article, blurbs on upcoming events and performers, cultural reviews, columns on the arts and neighborhood news.

With the exception of a handful of long-running columns—Hot Type, The Straight Dope, Neighborhood News, Hitsville and The Culture Club—virtually every section of *The Reader* is open to freelance writers, who contribute everything from lengthy cover stories to theater, book and film reviews to personal profiles.

Editor Michael Lenehan strongly urged journalists who want to write for *The Reader* to start with shorter pieces for the Our Town and Calendar sections. Articles in these sections average about 850 words and should take two to three days to research and write. *The Reader's* cover stories average 7,000 to 10,000 words.

Lenehan attributes *The Reader* diversity and offbeat quality to the paper being "open to new styles and voices—new people, young people, inexperienced people and people who are only going to have one story to tell in their whole lives."

Most articles are written on speculation, and stories are rarely assigned. "With writers whose work you don't know, it's impossible to tell from a query letter whether you're going to get a good read," said Lenehan. "So for that reason, we don't make any promises."

Before pitching a story idea or submitting an article, writers are urged to familiarize themselves thoroughly with the paper's style and contents.

Query letters are preferred over telephone calls from writers who feel it necessary to run their story idea by an editor first to see if there is any interest. Lenehan said he loathes queries that are broad and include only a general topic. Editors are usually willing to help writers hone a relatively focused story idea.

*The Reader* typically pays $125 for a Calendar story, $210 for an Our Town entry and up to $1,400 for a front-page feature article. Lenehan said the paper rarely pays kill fees, and stories are generally purchased for one-time rights.

The lead time for articles is two to three weeks, but an article submitted on a Monday can conceivably run in that Thursday's paper, Lenehan said. Submissions can be on a disk or hard copy.

A copy of the publication's editorial guidelines can be obtained by writing or calling *The Reader*'s offices.

The *Chicago Tribune* is the largest daily newspaper in the Chicago area with a weekday circulation of roughly 725,000 and a Sunday circulation of 1.1 million. While the *Tribune* is primarily a general-interest newspaper, it also includes "special interest" sections that run once a week and rely heavily on freelance contributions.

The feature sections offer the greatest opportunity for freelance writers. They include Tempo, The Arts, Friday, Transportation, Home, Real Estate, WomanNews, Travel, Your Place and the Sunday magazine. The *Tribune*'s zoned sections for Lake, DuPage and Will counties and the northwest suburbs are produced almost entirely by freelance writers. But the editors prefer to use journalists who are familiar with what's going on in those communities.

The *Tribune* has a full-time staff of roughly 600 writers and therefore rarely uses freelancers to cover national and foreign news or write for the Chicagoland section, according to John Twohey, a former senior editor who is now on a special task force at the newspaper.

Twohey said exceptions to this general policy are sometimes made. "If somebody writes or calls me and says, 'Here's a story I'd like to do, and I have connections in this community.' If I can be sold on your unique ability to tell the story to our audience, I will open the door for you."

The paper also accepts commentaries to fill the left column of the Tempo section when Bob Greene takes time off. The First Person column in the Sunday magazine is the domain of two or three writers who have longstanding relationships with the Tribune and, therefore, is mostly off-limits to new freelance writers.

Twohey said the *Tribune's* feature editors are open to stories that express a point of view. "We're looking less and less for objectivity in our feature pages," he said. "We want writers to tip their hands about their attitudes, about the people they are profiling, the phenomenon they are writing about."

Freelance writers are urged to send a query letter and clips. The query should include a paragraph or two explaining who you are and why you are qualified to tell the story. A follow-up call is acceptable if an editor fails to respond to your query within one to two weeks. Getting published in one section of the *Tribune* enhances a writer's prospects of being published elsewhere in the paper, Twohey said.

The *Tribune* generally pays $150 for one-time rights to an article of about 800 words. Writers are paid between $1,000 to $1,500 for a cover story that runs in the Sunday magazine. Twohey said that while freelance budgets vary slightly at each feature department, freelance rates at the *Tribune* are for the most part non-negotiable.

Articles for the Tempo section are due one week prior to publication. The lead time for most other feature sections is two to three weeks. The preferred method of submitting a story is by either modem or on disk. Writer's guidelines can be obtained by writing or calling the editor's office at the feature department you wish to write for.

*Crain's Chicago Business* is a weekly tabloid geared primarily toward business executives. In addition to covering breaking news, Crain's coverage includes company profiles, articles on industry trends and tips on after-work activities.
"We are a weekly, so we're trying to tell people bigger things than Biff and Betty starting up their own business," said Glenn Coleman, deputy managing editor at *Crain's*. "I gets lots of pitches for stories like that. Those stories are a dime a dozen, nothing really special."
Coleman said the TakeOut section, which is written almost entirely by freelancers, offers the best opportunity for non-staff writers. The TakeOut section is a supplement with articles on a number of issues surrounding a different subject or theme. Topics include environmental management, retirement planning, computerization and executive travel.
Freelance writers should contact the TakeOut editor to find out what topics will be covered in upcoming issues and then send a query letter with three to four solid story ideas that the paper has not covered in the past two years.
The inside-the-book and Options sections are two other fertile departments for freelancers. Inside-the-book stories are usually 20 to 30 inches of type and include company profiles and articles on business meetings and entrepreneurial ventures. The Options section includes 10- to 12-inch feature stories which focus primarily on after-work activities, including theater reviews, and blurbs on new products and gift ideas.
Coleman strongly urged writers to study the kinds of articles *Crain's* publishes before approaching the paper. "We want strong points of view that explain to very busy readers almost how to think about something," he said, "whether it's one company, an industry or a trend in the service sector."
Writers should send a resume, clips and a one-page query. Those with "weak" resumes will be asked to write the story on speculation, he said.
*Crain's* pays a flat fee of $165 for Options stories and $12.50 per column inch for other articles. TakeOut articles are assigned three months in advance.

*Chicago* magazine is a monthly publication that includes at least one or two in-depth feature articles on topics as varied as mayoral politics, health clubs, Chicago nightlife, beleaguered educators and the singles scene. Every issue generally includes a personality profile, theater and film reviews, as well as columns on art, business and the media.
Freelance opportunities are comparatively limited because the magazine comes out only 12 times a year and generally uses only one or two freelance-written feature stories per issue. Managing editor Joanne Trestrail, who has since left the magazine, noted that the *Chicago Tribune* publishes more copy in one week than *Chicago* magazine does in one year.
The Frontlines section offers the best bet for freelance journalists who want to write for *Chicago* magazine. Frontlines consist of short pieces averaging about

200 words on both well-known and obscure Chicagoans who are "doing something new and something interesting. "A novelist, casting director, soap-opera writer and masseuse are some of the people who have been spotlighted in the past. While Frontlines generally focuses on people, it also includes entries on historical events, new business ventures and emerging trends.

Freelance writers should send clips, if they have any, and a query letter demonstrating familiarity with the subject. Journalists who do not have clips are asked to write articles on speculation.

"Mechanics are not important, connections are not important," Trestrail said. "What's important is writing, having good ideas and executing them."

Trestrail advises people who want to write for the magazine to review at least two years of back issues. "I don't like when people ask, 'What are you looking for?'" she said. "The stuff that we're looking for is well-written stories on important subjects."

Chicago magazine pays between $100 and $300 for most Frontlines pieces and up to $4,000 for lengthy, in-depth feature articles. Writers are paid on acceptance. The lead time for articles is six to eight weeks.

Trestrail concluded her presentation with a remark that should hearten journalists who may at times feel overwhelmed by the seeming flood of competition in the local freelance market. "There are lots of writers in the world, but I think there aren't too many good ones, so you shouldn't be discouraged by the numbers," she said.

# Salt on the Wound

## ...What's in Your Hair and Other Tricks for Coming Up with Journalistic Story Ideas, Especially for, but Not Only, the Self-Absorbed

By S.L. Wisenberg

For a few days, I had a sore in my mouth from accidentally biting my inner whatsit—inner mouth? Mouth lining? Inner lip? I left it alone and it didn't get any better. I stopped by a drug store and found a tube of ointment for about $6. I thought it was silly to pay that much to heal a small sore that was bound to go away on its own—even though it hadn't as of yet. So I left the tube on the rack and later that night went to my neighborhood health-food store. There I found that the appropriate ointments and liquids were even more expensive. I talked to the drug-like-items salesperson.

Just put a little sea salt on there a few times a day, she said.

Really?

So I went home, put sea salt on my wound and it healed.

Why am I telling you this?

Because it's an example, albeit mundane, of how we're all living inside story ideas. Usable ones.

I came up with several from this admittedly teeny-tiny experience:

Trend: As people become skeptical of the medical establishment and the side effects of allopathic medicine, they turn more and more to "natural" treatments and health-food store potions for what ails them. (What needs to come next is a lot of research and reporting to check out the hypothesis. But you knew that.)

Or: They are turning to health-food store personnel to help them. Attendant questions: What kinds of things do people seek treatment for? What are the ethics? Who is this health food "pharmacist" or healer? What are the limits?

Or: the uses of salt. (Cleans your teeth. Cleans cast-iron pans. And how's Morton International—formerly Morton Thiokol, of the Challenger disaster—doing these days?)

Or: first-aid treatments you have in your kitchen.

Or: what the first-aid kit of the '90s should contain.

Yes, dear writer, you can be inordinately interested in yourself and still come up with ideas for stories that other people will read and, more importantly, that editors will pay you for. Or promise to pay you for. But that's another issue, dealt with elsewhere.

You can examine yourself and generate ideas from here till doomsday, even if you're eccentric and introspective. The following exercise should be helpful to anybody who wants to map out new story ideas—for any medium.

You'll need several plain pieces of paper and writing implements. Unless you have tiny handwriting, use an oversized sheet of paper. Or a sophisticated computer that makes pictures and has a huge screen.

On the first page, right in the middle, draw a human figure. (You.) Draw it in detail, even if you can't draw. Or cut out a picture of a body from the newspaper or a magazine. Make sure there's plenty of white space around the figure.

Then start at the top. Draw a line to your hair (or scalp) and put whatever comes to mind about your own hair. Do you think about dyeing your hair red but you're worried about reports of carcinogens? Jot that down. Some readers, somewhere are concerned, too. What dyes are safe? Can the average person buy them or are they available only to professional stylists?

Do you wonder if straight, ironed hair will come back in style?

You remember reading several years ago about hair analysis to determine nutritional deficiencies, and a judge who was interested in trying this to determine if a deficiency was causing behavioral problems in a juvenile offender. Are any reformers, psychologists, et al. using hair analyses in rehabilitation plans? What is going on in rehabilitation, anyway, in this era of shrinking funds and overcrowded prisons?

And by the way, speaking of hair and crime (pubic hair on a woman's underwear, wasn't it?), what about Gary Dotson? What is he doing now? Is it time for a "What ever happened to...?" Are there similar cases that are less publicized? Maybe check with the state's attorney's office...

You get the idea, right? Keep at it, not forgetting blood and inner organs. Keep moving down.

And speaking of feet, my first story for the *Miami Herald* was about old people's feet. I got the idea from walking around and seeing a lot of...old people's feet. The highlight of my reporting was the time I spent sitting in on a podiatrist's appointments. A patient in her 80s came into the examining room and handed him a plastic bag. In it were her corns. She had cut them off herself.

Once you've finished inventorying yourself as Body, it's time to move on. You also belong to groups, from condo association to World Association of Baying Journalists, and you have, as they say, a family of origin. Draw yourself in the midst of these and start drawing lines and making notes. Say that you have trouble when it comes to buying presents for your nephew. Let's assume that you're childless and this particular problem comes merely from not spending much time with children.

Is this a common problem? (Ask toy-store salespeople.) How could you solve it? (You could figure out in advance what he'd like. Months before holidays, ask his parents, ask him to show you his toys and ask which ones he plays with the most, etc.) You could write a tidy service piece for a magazine read mostly by childless people in the new aunt/uncle age group. Or new grandparents.

For deep issues, you're on your own. I'm sure they'll come to mind; there's a raft of psychologists and other experts for comments on various family dynamics.

When you're through with self in Groups, you're ready for self as Consumer, Employee, Citizen, Traveler, Writer, Driver, Diner, Rabble-rouser, Penitent... Feel free to paste on to your sheets pictures of cars, stores, food and so on, so that you can chart your relationship with your car's tires, for example. (By now you should realize I'm not kidding.)

To keep from being overwhelmed by your fascinating world and self, pause after you finish each sheet and start cranking out query letters.

Thanks for bearing with me. And, no, I haven't bitten myself in the inner mouth for weeks now. Thanks for asking.

# The New Covenant

## Contracts Can Be Changed

*By Ron Dorfman*

Our text today is the Book of Exodus, chapter 33, verses 9 to 23. God is giving Moses the assignment to lead the people of Israel, but Moses, while flattered, doesn't agree immediately; he sees potential problems and wants to protect his own interests. So Moses and God haggle back and forth until they reach mutually acceptable terms.

Really. You could look it up. Now, if those guys could make such significant trade-offs, there's no reason for you to think that the boilerplate on a standard magazine contract is carved on stone tablets. Everything is negotiable.

Editors, or most of them anyway, are not inclined to be legalistic, and neither should you be. What's called for is a friendly, businesslike recognition of the mutual interest in avoiding unnecessary hassles, producing a good magazine on time, and establishing or preserving the writer-editor relationship.

That means, among other things, negotiating only what's important to you. Your opus on the best little cheesecake in Chicago is not likely to become a movie starring Dolly Parton, so arguing about subsidiary rights or work-made-for-hire clauses may not be worth the effort; but if you think you can market the piece to Pastry & Confections Week after its local appearance, then insist on your rights. Start by crossing out the offending language and writing in "First North American Serial rights only," with your initials, before returning the signed contract. If the editor insists on keeping "all rights" or the work-made-for-hire clause, then you should insist on a higher fee to compensate for lost potential income. (If the contract says nothing about rights, they're yours by law.)

You won't get what you don't ask for, and you should almost always ask for more money than the editor offers. Each writer will have his or her own calculus for deciding how much is too little for a given assignment. You have to be able to say—to yourself first and then to the editor—that to do a respectable job on that piece will take you at least X number of days or weeks, which should establish the minimum fee you are willing to accept. And you have to be prepared to say flatly and without rancor that you'd love to do this piece, but you just can't for that kind of money. This is a matter of long-term survival as well as self-respect.

You might suggest the name of a young writer who perhaps would be willing to take the assignment. If the editor has any leeway (most do, some don't), she'll sweeten the pot.

Even when the offer is higher than your minimum, it cannot hurt to ask for more: "Geez, I know times are hard at Engulf & Devour, but couldn't you do a little better than that? How about if we skip the lunch at Avanzare?..." Or: "That's what you were paying five years ago. If you guys haven't had a raise since then, OK, I understand. But my rent keeps going up..." An offer of $1,000 can magically turn into $1,200 or $1,500.

But if you're facing starvation, take what you can get—and then take a realistic look at your career.

The kill fee is standard boilerplate and not easily negotiated the first time you work for a magazine, unless you're a well-established writer. But the second time you take an assignment, you should strike the kill-fee provision before returning the contract, again affixing your initials.

If the editor objects, remind him he's already seen you in action and you are no longer trying out; you'll work with him to get a good fix on the kind of piece that's expected and that's what you'll deliver, but not without a guarantee of being paid in full: "If you're not confident I can do this job, or if you just want to hedge your bets in case the idea turns out to be not really workable, then you should find somebody else to experiment on."

A writer facing starvation probably won't want to go to the wall on this, but should at least make the show of initially striking the provision from the contract. Established and successful writers should always refuse to work under a kill-fee provision as a matter of conscience and of solidarity with those who are struggling. Editors must be made to feel embarrassed and guilty about this thing.

Eliminating the kill-fee almost eliminates the concept of "acceptance" of a manuscript, and that is threatening to an editor's identity. You need to make clear that you know the value of good editing and would like as much of it as possible. Most contracts don't say anything about rewrites. In your letter accepting the contract with modifications, you should say that you'd like an early conference once you have some idea of how the piece is taking shape, to make sure you are operating in sync.

If it seems reasonable to you given the deadline and dimensions of the piece, offer to show the editor an early draft. This will simultaneously score you Brownie points and establish the very important point that the manuscript you turn in on deadline is not to be treated as a first draft. And then be explicit: "After submission of the manuscript, I'll be happy to fill any holes you identify, and to do one major rewrite if requested before (date: two to four weeks after deadline). I will do later or additional rewrites for $XXX each."

Also in your cover letter, you may want to reserve the right to approve the final edit. As the *New York Times* correction box reminds us daily, about half of all errors in published copy are introduced by editing. Try something tactful like: "No offense intended, but I reserve the right to review the final edited version and to withdraw my byline if we cannot agree on changes."

You should try to establish a definite date for payment. Contract clauses that provide for payment "on acceptance" or "on publication" are unacceptable. Strike them and write in "not later than (date)," indicating 30 days after delivery, or maybe the last day of the month in which the assignment is due. If the editor demurs—and she will—affect the voice of sweet reason and point out that you have agreed to provide a service by a specific date, and she should in all fairness agree to provide payment by a specific date. You're on shaky ground here if you have not performed on deadline in previous assignments, but otherwise this is something you ought to insist on.

The proffered contract may or may not have language dealing with expenses. If it doesn't, or if it states that the publisher will not cover expenses, you should talk with the editor about how the reporting is to be accomplished. If it involves nothing but local phone calls and a bus ride or two, don't sweat it. But if the editor agrees (or insists) that more substantial out-of-pocket costs will have to be incurred to produce a respectable piece of reporting, one way around the dilemma is to estimate the costs and increase the article fee accordingly (including an increment to cover the taxes on the extra "income").

If the editor can't or won't do this, you have three choices: reject the assignment; accept it with the explicit caveat that the piece will not represent your best work; or, if the assignment looks too good for either of those alternatives, pay your own expenses—at least they're deductible.

Even if the boilerplate does provide for timely payment of "reasonable and necessary expenses," and the assignment looks as if it's going to involve cabs, messengers, database research, interview lunches, long-distance calls, or flights on the Concorde, you'll want to talk to the editor about what limits there are on expenses and whether he can provide an advance if you need one. Then put your understanding in writing in your cover letter. One actual dispute involved a New York travel editor refusing to believe that a modest dinner for two at one of Chicago's trendy restaurants could be as pricey as dinner in New York, so be as specific as possible about likely costs.

A final tip: Writing for magazines is not a privilege. It's a business.

# It's Your Problem

## Finding Compatibility with Your Editor's Computer System

*By Betty Sherwood*

In the early '80s, when I was working in the computer department of a large corporation, the employees grumbled about not being able to get at data because it was on the "wrong" computer. "Can't," they said, tossing out such terms as "not compatible," "wrong word length," "byte size," "check bits," "blocking," "file types" and "no cabling."

Things haven't changed much.

A writer buys an IBM-compatible computer with 5¼" DS/DD diskette drive and WordPerfect to get compatibility with 10 of the 12 publications the writer regularly sells to and all's well. Hah! One month later, the publishing company that provides 40 percent of the writer's income scraps their two-year-old computers and buys new 486s with 3½" drives. This means the writer must part with some of those "big earnings" to regain compatibility with that publisher.

It may strike some writers as odd and unfair that the compatibility issue should be theirs rather than the publisher's. It is, but no more odd and unfair than many other publisher/writer transactions. Editors and publishers were dragged, kicking and screaming, into the computer era by writers. It took editors 10 years to be convinced that accepting stories on computer files would be more economical and enable them to publish faster. Once they were convinced, getting computer files to them became the writers' problems.

So exactly what do editors do about compatibility? Complain.

One editor, speaking at an event sponsored by the Chicago Book Clinic several year ago, complained about writers submitting diskettes in incompatible formats from incompatible computers. After the program, I told her there was an inexpensive software program that would translate most or all of these diskettes to her standard, and, if she would call me later, I would look up the address, etc. for her. She never called. She wanted the writers to solve her problem. She didn't want to deal with the damned computer. And she is not unique. Most editors are intimidated by computers.

So writers must try to achieve compatibility with every editor's favorite software. This is expensive and time-consuming. In addition, total compatibility is not possible. But we can at least give them files.

First, a writer must decide where to attack a particular file transfer/incompatibility problem: machine type, diskette type or file type.

The most common type of machine compatibility problem is Macintosh versus PC compatible (including IBM Micro Channel). Possible solutions are: use diskettes to transfer the files (aided by software), transfer the files via a modem or carry your computer into the editor's office and use LapLink from Traveling Software (to transfer between PCs) and LapLink Mac (to go from Mac to Mac or PC to Mac) to move the files to the editor's computer via cable.

The editor decides which method of transfer you must use. Some editors insist you use MCI Mail or the mail feature on a Bulletin Board Service (BBS) or a direct modem link to transfer your file. MCI Mail is pay-by-the-year plus usage. Three of the larger BBSs are CompuServe, Prodigy and Online America. And most, if not all, are interconnected so you can be a CompuServe subscriber and leave a message or file for someone who has only an MCI Mail account. On-line America, Prodigy, CompuServe and other BBSs and MCI Mail have 800 numbers, and remember to ask questions about sending things to people on other services before you subscribe.

CompuServe cannot be used by a sane person without the aid of CompuServe Information Manager (CIM), purchased separately, or any other "front end" that gives you a better than .001 percent chance of figuring out how to get anything done on CompuServe. However, CIM, not the greatest front-end in the world, may not work with your computer/modem; it didn't work with mine, and, as I said, CompuServe is functionally useless without a front-end.

The other solution, direct file transfer, has the same basic requirement as a BBS and MCI Mail: a modem and modem software. You really need a separate software communications package to run the modem with the least possible frustration. With direct file transfer, you have to connect with the publisher and send (rather than upload) the file under your own steam. This is not always as simple as it sounds. In fact, I have failed when I had a programmer on the other end.

If publishers wanted to be nice to writers, they would buy ProComm Plus, or any other modem software package that includes something called Host mode, which would allow the editor's computer to act as a BBS. If you are transferring or uploading large files for PC-compatibles, you can use PKZIP (from PKWare) to compress them and reduce your phone costs. Some modems also do compression for you.

If you are sending a Zipped file or a word processing file, use Xmodem, Kermit or any other file type—the same type on both ends. For ASCII files only, you can use ASCII. Although this is all learnable (particularly with the aid of the excellent ProComm Plus manual), it can be difficult when one-half of the problem is sitting on the editor's desk, and the editor hands off the whole problem to the writer.

If you have an editor who insists on a diskette, you may have another compatibility problem. For example, if you are a PC user, you may have a 5$\frac{1}{4}$" drive, which writes only to 360k diskettes, while the editor has a 3$\frac{1}{2}$" high-density drive. Solution: buy a drive. They cost less than $75, come in ultrathin sizes so even if you have no open external bays (places where the small panel on the front comes off so you can install something in the space behind and access it from the front), you can pull your old drive and replace it with two new drives.

However, if you have anything less than a 286 (8086 or 8088 are both "less than" a 286), the file-transfer rate built into the machine won't handle a high density drive. Even if you have a 286 or higher, you must have DOS version 3.3 or higher. There is a very small chance that even if you have a 286 and can add a new drive, you might have to buy a new controller card to handle it. You might also have to run the setup program to tell the computer that there is another drive in there.

If you aren't sure about all this, take the technical description (manual) of your computer or the model number information stamped on the back with you to the computer store. You may also need the hard-drive type, which should be displayed as one of the first text activities when you turn on the computer or be available through one of the utilities provided with the computer.

If you make all this information available to computer salespeople, they should be able to provide a compatible drive or new card/drive combination that will handle whatever your setup requires. There are no exact guidelines on all this because computer manufacturers are always busy, busy, busy making everything incompatible with everything else. For total compatibility with all editors, you need a high density $5^{1}/_{4}$" drive and a high-density $3^{1}/_{2}$" drive.

A $5^{1}/_{4}$" (or $3^{1}/_{2}$") high-density drive can format and then write to low-density diskettes so you get two for the price of one. Check the FORMAT command instructions in your DOS manual or buy utility software (Norton Utilities, PC Tools).

Be careful about using a high-density drive to write to a diskette that was formatted as low density on another computer. Reason: there is a tiny head writing to a larger channel, and the head in another drive may be calibrated with just enough difference so it writes in a different place within that wide channel.

After a few writes by different computers, the computer you use may not be able to zero in on the "writing" you want to access. Result: read failure, which is not something you want to send to an editor. Therefore, reformat diskettes (especially low-density diskettes) before you use them if you got them from someone else with data on them. And to be extra careful, use a bulk eraser (electromagnetic field generator), which you can buy at Radio Shack. But use it sparingly, and always use it well away from the computer.

Installing a drive is as easy as any other screwing and fixing chore. The only difference is you have to be careful of static electricity. I stand on a static mat in my bare feet. Others keep a bare foot up against a metal chair leg. The techie simply grounds herself by touching the metal of the computer case with both hands, and then makes sure she doesn't move her feet at all on the carpet. Without this precaution, static electricity can zap your motherboard or other vital chip and this is *expensive*.

What about sending diskettes if you have a Mac and the editor has a PC? If the editor has a $3^{1}/_{2}$" drive, you are OK. Otherwise, you need a friend with a PC to get from $3^{1}/_{2}$" to $5^{1}/_{4}$". The Mac and PC do have different formats, but all drives are just spinning platters with a read/write head. This means the actual format or quantity of data on the diskette (depending on drive capabilities and diskette manufacturer's density specs) is determined by software which controls the actions of the read/write head. There are at least two software packages that allow DOS people to create or read a Mac diskette; the cost is around $60 for the DOS version. You have to use high density 3½" diskettes for the PC.

And the Mac operating system (System 7 or later) allows Mac people to read or write a DOS diskette. You need a Mac superdrive (on all Macs sold after 1990). The problem is most Mac people can't find it. It isn't loaded during the normal installation procedure. You will find it on the System Tidbits diskette; it's called the Apple File Exchange. However, it is difficult to use and you may want to buy a product that provides a better interface, such as PC Exchange or Access PC. Both products have additional translation capabilities. If you want to use Apple File Exchange without the add-on, you may need to buy a book to help you use it.

When reading files from a PC diskette into a Mac, the word processing software may be all you need. WordPerfect for the Mac, I'm told, reads DOS diskettes and writes to them (when they have already been formatted on a DOS machine). Again, you'll have to get the particulars from the software company or the manual. One problem you may run into is forks. You see, the Apple Mac splits file information into two forks: a data fork, which contains the data, and a resource fork, which has information about the program that created the file, some of the formatting and icon information, etc. You may not need that second fork for your file to be readable on the Mac side. And many of the programs involved in a transfer will supply it: communications programs on the Mac side, Mac-In-Dos, LapLink Mac and even some of the file-translation programs discussed later provide a diskette for the Mac side with the forks. In Mac to DOS transfer, the second fork is combined with the first, or dumped. If your editor is used to working with files that have their own icons, you may need that second fork.

What if you have an old clunker? A company called Intersecting Concepts once made Media Master to allow reading and writing of multitudinous diskette types (and may still sell it), but they aren't currently findable—if in fact they still exist.

Now we're down to the last compatibility problem: file type. Each word processing package has its own. If you use an ASCII (the PC vanilla file type) file viewer/editor to look at the files created by WordPerfect, for example, you can see the words, but among the words are lots of weird symbols. These—the file headers, file-end markers, line feeds and many other file attributes—are different for each word processing package. So what is the solution if you have WordPerfect and your editor uses XyWrite? File conversion software.

Most word processing packages offer limited conversion, and all offer ASCII—but that is the choice of last resort. Two file conversion products are Software Bridge from Systems Compatibility Corp. in Chicago and Word-for-Word from MasterSoft. Word-for-Word had a big bug in the DisplayWrite conversion, and I got angry (I needed the conversion *now*) and bought Software Bridge—which has more file types available, but is harder to use.

These packages aren't expensive (as conversion solutions go) and are very important for most writers. But you usually have to update this software whenever you or your editor updates word processing software because the developers change the file attributes almost every time they update or "improve" their programs.

If you have WordPerfect for Windows, and your editor has DOS WordPerfect, you can transfer WordPerfect files freely as long as you don't use things like m-dashes or real quotes (from the upper ASCII/ANSI character set). If you use the WordPerfect printer installation rather than the Windows printer controller, there is no problem.

The WordPerfect Mac version is also the same file type, and the files should be compatible. But you may need to use conversion software for that transfer also. (WordPerfect says as long as you stick to simple text and Courier fonts, there is no problem.)

All flavors of MS Word on both the PC side and the Mac side are very compatible, and you don't need a converter for that transfer. Check with the tech support people or sales for compatibilities of any other package.

If the editor's word processing software is so incredibly obscure that it isn't available as a conversion, or if the update to the conversion software is a month or two or three behind the word processing software changes, you may be stuck sending ASCII files. ASCII (sometimes called DOS text) is the PC standard, and ANSI is the Windows standard. All the typewriter characters are the same in both "standards"—they don't diverge until you hit the upper ASCII/ANSI character sets (m-dashes, etc.).

Another file type, EBCDIC, is IBM's standard from their mainframe and mini—they used it for DisplayWrite, too. Therefore, most word processing software offers EBCDIC conversion for this one company's needs.

With an ASCII conversion you lose the bold, underline, etc., and in most ASCII conversions, each soft return (the character that allows word-wrap to control line endings) is converted to a hard return. So anyone reading an ASCII file into a word-processing program must get rid of all the hard returns to allow their software to control the line wrap. They also have to get rid of the spaces (tab characters are converted to an appropriate number of spaces). It's easy, but the fix is on the editor's end, and they often can't quite grasp it. All they have to do is use the search-and-replace feature of their word processing software with or without "approve," and starting after the title, replace all hard returns with a space. Then, they have to reset the paragraphs by searching and replacing all instances of five spaces in a row (if you had your paragraph tab set to indent five spaces) with a hard return followed by a tab.

The result is no hard returns except for paragraph endings and no spaces where tab characters should be. If you have numbered or bulleted items in your story, you'll have to figure out another algorithm to pick these up. So be prepared for the editor's whine, and be free with hand-holding instructions.

What is the cost to you, the individual, underpaid writer, to achieve compatibility with 10–100 different editors? Estimate $75 for each drive, another $100–$200 if you need a controller card, $75 for each conversion package you need, $100–$400 for a good modem and $60 for modem software.

Each editor could buy this equipment and software and be compatible with scores of writers, but they prefer that writers drop the bucks and figure it all out. And people wonder why writers drink.

# Going to Small Claims Court

## Judges Care Less About a Writer's Precious Prose Than the Words in a Signed Contract

*By Keith Watson*

Writers pay so much attention to the words they create, yet so little to the words in the contracts they sign. Why is this? Do we have a collective allergy to legal procedures? Ever since I covered court cases in my first newspaper job, I vowed never to go to court myself. I found the process tiresome, expensive and embarrassing for everyone. Even the attorneys and judges seemed bored and irritated by the formal procedures and delays.

But working in the magazine business drove me to break my vow. After receiving my third kill fee—a measly $467.50 rather than the $1,750.00 that I deserved after six weeks of research and writing, I protested my treatment loudly. First I went through the proper channels: writing a polite but firm letter to the magazine and filing a grievance with the National Writers Union (NWU). I then played my final card: filing suit in Small Claims Court.

I'm proud of what I did, but I didn't win—which again demonstrated to me the precariousness of being a freelancer. The judge didn't take the time to judge the quality of my research or writing. His bottom line was the precise wording in the contract I'd signed.

■ ■ ■

To understand what drove me to court, let me describe two previous times when my articles were killed:

■ *Houston City* magazine (now defunct) asked me to write a 2,500-word advertorial for $900 about northwest Houston. The assistant publisher accepted it but called a week later to say she had to kill it because the magazine wasn't able to sell enough ads. I received a quarter of the fee—$225, as the contract stipulated.

■ A few months later, the editor-in-chief of the same magazine asked me to write a 1,500-word profile of a rival publisher who produced a *Texas Town & Country* clone called *Ultra*. The assignment seemed dubious but I trusted the editor, who had given me the green light for my first successful magazine feature, "The Snoop Sisters," which tattled on Houston's gossip columnists. I wrote a profile that the editor accepted but, a week later, he was deposed by the publisher and two senior editors, who killed my piece. I received only $150, a quarter of the $600 I had been promised.

My freelance career went relatively smoothly for the next few years. The next disastrous period, however, began in 1990. After I had written my (unpublished) profile, a friend of mine was appointed editor of the magazine, and he asked me to assemble a health-care section. Despite its apparent affluence, *Ultra* had a shaky history and I feared I wouldn't get paid. Nevertheless, I agreed to help my overworked friend. I turned in the section on time and relocated from Houston to the Midwest. *Ultra* published all of my articles with minimal editing. Then I learned that the editor had been fired. I telephoned long-distance day after day to ask for payment. I finally received a check, but it bounced. So did the next one.

While I was awaiting payment of nearly $4,000 from *Ultra*, some of which I owed to subcontractors, I started work on my first piece for *Chicago* magazine. I had submitted some appealing story ideas—a feature called "Underground Chicago," pitched two years before the Great Chicago Flood—but I was assigned one of the editor-in-chief's stodgy ideas: a 3,500-word piece on financial services, an obvious ploy to drum up advertising revenue.

I was specifically asked to write about six complex subjects—banking, brokerage services, insurance and tax advice, as well as real estate and legal services (the latter two aren't usually considered part of the personal-finances realm). The editor-in-chief's working title was "Getting More for Less," an omen of how *Chicago* magazine would treat me, the freelancer.

It had been a few years since I had received a kill fee, so I signed *Chicago*'s standard contract without thinking. I would earn $1,750.00 if the piece were accepted; $437.50 if not. Here I was again, pathetic Charlie Brown running to kick a football held in place by spiteful Lucy van Pelt.

I spent six weeks reading, conducting 20 interviews, writing and rewriting. A senior editor asked me to sectionalize the article, writing 600 words on each on the six topics. As an example, she cited the factoid style of a feature called "Fast Chicago," which the magazine had published several months earlier.

The more I researched, the more I realized the impossibility of this assignment. One couldn't cover any of these subjects effectively in 600 words, particularly when one considered (a) the wide range in age of *Chicago*'s readers (b) their varying tolerance for financial risk and (c) the recession just starting. I worked hard, however, and did my best. I turned in the article on time, and the senior editor called the next day to thank me for a "comprehensive" piece.

The next I heard from her, however, was in a terse letter received two-and-a-half weeks later, blaming me for not following the story outline (I did, much too closely) and telling me I'd receive a kill fee. She also apologized: "I'm sorry that I gave you the impression that it [the article] was fine."

I was devastated. Because of the battle with *Ultra*, the stress of moving to Chicago and the latest mess with *Chicago,* I broke down in tears. At age 36, I felt too old to be hazed again, especially after I'd proven myself by writing cover stories for other magazines and being published steadily for 15 years.

When the January 1991 issue of *Chicago* came out, I read the financial-services piece. It was obvious the new writer had been told to refocus the piece, which was no longer segmented and omitted real estate and legal services. I was livid. Since the editor-in-chief had since departed (not a surprise in the turnstile

world of magazines), I wrote to the publisher and asked for full payment.
The publisher responded that anything the editors had told me was "irrelevant." She rejected my demand for full payment, and her arrogance fueled my search for justice. Publishers live off the sweat of writers to fill the pages between cigarette, fashion and liquor ads, and they think writers should labor vainly in the service of "art." Well, *Chicago* magazine is not art: it's commerce, and writing an article on personal finance is commercial work. Moreover, it's unfair to cheat a writer of 75 percent of the fee for work that he or she has been explicitly asked to do. It's like asking a plumber to build a pink bathroom and then, after the work is finished, complaining the fixtures aren't blue and refusing to pay the full bill.

With documentation in hand, I asked for help from the NWU Grievance Committee. After two rounds of letters to the new editor, however, the magazine refused to budge. Michael Miner, the Reader's "Hot Type" columnist, brought the controversy to public view in the January 23, 1992 issue.

## Enough Is Enough

Kill fees turned me into an activist. I filed my case on Writers' Rights Day in June 1992, and fellow NWU members Judith Cooper and Betty Sherwood came along to lend moral support. Because my requested damages of $1,300 exceeded the Pro Se Court limit, I filed in Small Claims Court, which had a $2,500 ceiling. (The filing fees for Small Claims Court are similar to those described below for Pro Se Court.)

As is my habit, I saved all documentation, including copies of my contract, the two-page story outline, a copy of the senior editor's letter accusing me of not following the outline, a copy of my letter to the publisher and her response, and correspondence between the NWU and *Chicago*'s new editor.

The court schedule moved swiftly. I filed in early June and the defendants asked for a continuance. The judge refused to grant *Chicago* a second continuance, so the trial took place in early October. The weeks between my filing and the trial gave me time to prepare.

If you don't hire an attorney, make sure to rehearse beforehand with friends. An attorney friend, James P. Crawley, offered objective advice, and his participation gave me the satisfaction of showing someone from outside the media what a corrupt mess the magazine business is. Because of rehearsing with him, I was able to state the chronology of events succinctly and without malice during the case. Ron Dorfman, a former editor of *Chicago* and a grievance officer of NWU Chicago, testified that I had followed the outline and deserved the full amount.

Nevertheless, I lost. The judge based his ruling on the wording in *Chicago*'s standard contract. This was, after all, Small Claims Court and a judge handles many cases each day. He didn't pore over my draft and compare it to the outline or the published piece. He wasn't about to set precedent and rule that kill fees were abusive and unfair. In fact, he called *Chicago* a "prestigious" magazine and lamented his inability to get published in law journals. He didn't grasp that my situation was different from that of an attorney wanting to enhance his reputation by being published in a professional journal. But it was too late to respond—case closed and by law I couldn't appeal (although *Chicago* could have if I had won).

I've mulled over what I might have said or not said. But after a few days of hand-wringing, I concluded that my attorney and I did virtually everything that we could have done. We were defeated by the words in the contract, which stipulated that *Chicago* magazine could kill my manuscript if "unusable." Any reasonable person would have judged it usable, but the judge ruled that the contract gave *Chicago* the ultimate say.

Other writers have told me that a different judge might have ruled in my favor. Had I sued *Houston City,* perhaps, for either of the cases in which my articles were killed, I probably would have stood a better chance of winning. But I have my doubts. When a judge holds a signed contract giving the publisher the option to pay only a quarter of the fee, the writer's position is weak. That's one reason why the NWU advises its members to use its Standard Journalism Contract. It avoids kill fees and calls for one fee, one use; full payment on submission of contracted work; and arbitration of disputes.

### Court: The Last Resort

Always avoid going to court, but reserve it as the final step to show others that you mean business. There are several steps to take earlier—phone calls, letters, appeals from friends who work at the magazine, or more creative ideas, like a threat that I used to scare *Ultra*.

Not long after receiving my kill fee from *Chicago*, I phoned *Ultra*'s business manager and warned his secretary quite calmly that if I did not get a good check I would fax copies of *Ultra*'s bounced checks to every gossip reporter in Texas. To my delight, I got a certified check shipped overnight and was paid before the magazine folded. I settled the dispute without having to go to court.

Writers should take preventive measures as well. Had I signed a fair contract with *Chicago* in the first place, I wouldn't have found myself on the way to court. But in case you find yourself in a similar predicament, here are some tips for filing suit. Keep in mind, however, that the fee amounts and locations are subject to revision.

**Where to file:** Since my article covered legal services, I knew where to look for the filing papers. After passing through the metal detectors at Daley Center (on Randolph between Clark and Dearborn, with the Picasso sculpture out front), I went up to the sixth floor, where I picked up the necessary forms.

**Filing suit:** Most magazines are owned by corporations, and you need to track down the exact name of the business and address of the corporation's "agent for service of process." To obtain this information, go to a law library, ask an attorney-friend or call the corporations department (312-793-3380) of the Illinois Secretary of State.

**Representing yourself:** Most attorneys don't want to bother with Small Claims Court because there's little money in it. Not to worry. By representing yourself, you can look like the admirable "little guy." Take into account your temperament. If you're a do-it-yourselfer, consider filing *pro se* (a Latin expression, pronounced "pro-say," meaning "for yourself"), but don't expect a judge to be kind to courtroom novices.

**Do your homework:** Suing even in Small Claims Court is not easy because of the legalese. I suggest every writer buy a relevant handbook such as *Everybody's Guide to the Law* (Perennial Library, $14); Frank Free, NWU National Grievance Officer, recommends *Everybody's Guide to Small Claims Court* (Nolo Press, $15.95).

**Pro Se Court:** This is the smallest and most user-friendly of Cook County's courts. Unfortunately, the amount I was seeking—roughly $1,300—topped the Pro Se limit, which was raised from $1,000 to $1,500 shortly after I filed. The Office of the Circuit Court has a brief pamphlet that explains how to file suit, and the Pro Se staff (312-443-5626) in Room 602 of Daley Center helps plaintiffs start the process. It costs $40 to file for claims up to $250, $65 for claims up to $1,000 and $75 for claims up to $1,500.

**Additional fees:** You'll need to pay at least $2 to have a summons mailed by certified or registered mail. If you have a summons served in person by the Sheriff's Department (I did), it costs $23 plus mileage for each defendant.

**Copies, copies, copies:** Before arriving at the courthouse to file your complaint, make five copies of all the necessary papers and your contract, assuming you have one. Save all receipts because, if you win, the loser must pay your filing fees. As you prepare for your day in court, make at least three copies of all documents you plan to use as evidence: one set for yourself, one for the judge and one for the defense team.

### Writers Who Have Won

I've swapped court stories with a few NWU members. One won after the defendant failed to appear, but he doesn't expect to collect because the publisher has gone bankrupt. Another friend filed against two people who refused to pay her. In both cases, she was fighting not magazines but individuals who had asked her to write promotional materials. She won both times but found the process nerve-wracking. Even after winning one case, she had to file papers to garnish the wages of a physician who clearly could have afforded to pay her.

Another NWU writer won a case against a magazine that published her article (submitted "on spec") and never paid her. The magazine tried to exhaust her through appeals but she won final judgment. More recently, a San Francisco writer and NWU member won a case against the *Village Voice*. Even though the *Voice* is published in New York City, he filed suit in San Francisco and had lawyer-friends in Manhattan serve the papers. Rules vary by state, however, and

I have not heard of a Chicago writer suing an out-of-state publication. It seems plausible, however, that a magazine with advertising offices in Chicago or being sold on city newsstands could be sued in Cook County.

After being served, a defendant may call and say, "Gee, I had no idea this had gotten so out-of-hand. I'm writing a check for the full amount right now!" Then again, it's likely you're dealing with an editor with more denial skills than Richard Nixon and access to high-paid attorneys.

As the trial date approaches, you may get a compromise offer. I refused to accept *Chicago*'s $500 offer (in addition to the $437.50 kill fee) because I didn't want to accept gag-order restrictions routinely attached to out-of-court pacts. I wanted to make a stand about writers' rights.

• • •

Freelancers must become more assertive and learn to negotiate better contracts and higher pay. We are, after all, entrepreneurs, and bill collection is an important part of our business. To cover the costs of collection, we need to charge more for each assignment.

Without a doubt, suing is time-consuming, but winning is possible if a magazine has broken a contract tenet. Even losing a case may be worth it. At the very least, my relatively inexpensive lawsuit inconvenienced *Chicago*'s editors, and the publicity muddied the magazine's image. The case proved to me that *Chicago* would rather pay a high-priced attorney than treat a freelance writer fairly.

Filing suit also marked a turning point in my career. I no longer write "on spec," take on vague assignments or sign contracts with kill fees. Instead of continuing as a wimpy freelancer, I've become a more sensible, wary business person who happens to write for a living. While I hope not to file suit again, I'm ready if necessary.

As Marlon Brando, playing an attorney in the film *A Dry White Season* put it, "Justice and the law are distant cousins." To obtain justice, freelancers must pay more attention to contracts. We need to organize and work together to change the publishing industry's abusive practices.

# Two Views On Public Relations

## Working With Public Relations
### Sometimes You Have to Play the Game

By Len Strazewski

"I'd like to talk to you, but all interviews have to be approved by our public relations department. It's company policy."

Few things make a writer's teeth grind harder. You've reached the right source at the right time and you've got the right questions in mind—then you have to stop, contact a public relations person and explain yourself all over again.

Maybe you get back to your source; maybe you don't. Maybe you can still write the piece but not as well, or maybe you can't write it at all. Either way you've wasted time without advancing your research.

Public relations people can be a pain in the posterior. I know, because for a brief period in my career, I was one, fielding media calls on blessings to curses, materialism to spirituality, money to poverty.

My first job after journalism school at Northwestern University was as a press aide to John Cardinal Cody, Roman Catholic Archbishop of Chicago, one of the most controversial religious leaders ever to reign in the Chicago area. And reign he did, as a Prince of the Church and as the Corporation Sole of a billion-dollar institution that controlled hundreds of churches and one of the 10 largest school systems, public or private, in the United States.

Cardinal Cody was nothing if not colorful in his decision-making. I often received calls from reporters covering various protest marches in front of schools, churches or Archdiocesan offices. A City News Bureau reporter once called and said, "I'm writing a story about picketers in front of Holy Name Cathedral. They're saying that Cardinal Cody is a racist pig. Is this true?"

I told him that I didn't think so, but I wasn't going to ask the cardinal.

On another occasion, Pulitzer Prize-winning reporter Rob Warden, then with the *Chicago Daily News*, called and asked for a comment from Cardinal Cody about "revelations in the Church report."

I told him I didn't know which report he was referring to and he said, "The Church report. Don't you read newspapers?"

It turned out he was referring to a report issued by Sen. Frank Church who was then chairman of the Senate intelligence committee. The report had disclosed Federal Bureau of Investigation files that suggested that Cardinal Cody had agreed to help the FBI undermine activities of Rev. Martin Luther King. (Total crap, by the way.)

I pointed out to Warden that when somebody calls the Archdiocese of

Chicago and asks about churches, we don't immediately think of senators, and I hung up on him. When he called back, I politely told him that the cardinal said the report was nonsense and wouldn't dignify the question with an interview.

It was a fascinating 14 months for a 20-year-old breaking into Chicago media, but I guess I just wasn't a public relations kind of guy. I left the job shortly thereafter and I took with me an understanding of what PR people can and cannot do, and how to make the most of your unavoidable relationship.

First, and foremost, don't expect PR people to be great information sources. Sure, corporate and institutional public relations departments pump out reams of press releases; for the most, these handouts are completely worthless for news reporters and of minimal value to other writers. The tidbits that most PR departments distribute are commodity properties: personnel changes, required quarterly financial reports, new product announcements and the rare profile or feature that shows the company or institution in a positive light. One exception is the occasional survey or study generated by consulting companies or university think tanks that may provide interesting bits of factual data for more focused stories. PR staffs generate "factoids," not information.

And as a writer, you can also count on PR executives not to be great sources about controversial topics. Don't expect them to confirm that their boss is a racist, for example. They probably don't know and, if they did, they wouldn't say.

However, PR people do play an important and often helpful role to writers as native guides to their organizations—resources that can help writers survive in the institutional jungles of bureaucracy.

Since surviving my own PR days, I've specialized in business and technology reporting, writing articles about human resource management, corporate finance, insurance, employee benefits and information technology, all types of business esoterica. PR people have become extremely valuable to me in locating sources within their organizations, briefing me on areas of expertise and translating jargon. In short, if used correctly, PR people can provide access to information as often as they deny access.

I have no qualms, by the way, about going around PR departments when I know exactly which source serves the needs of my story. But to avoid the dreaded referral back to PR, I've found that it may be best to play a little of the corporate game—when I have time. Initiating the call to PR to set up an interview may save time in the long run.

And, by the way, I don't call to "request" an interview. I'm not asking, I'm telling. I just want their help in getting to the right person. Sometimes, PR people can actually get a better source than the writer expected—a person with more insight and ability than your intended source. It pays to say, "I was thinking that the corporate treasurer would be the best to comment on this, unless you can suggest someone better." Sometimes they can.

In my own PR job, I kept lists of sources who knew what they doing and who could sustain conversations without putting their feet in their mouths—something Cardinal Cody couldn't always manage. Once they've helped you locate a source, they can also help in scheduling an interview in a timely fashion. A good PR person can track down their executives—even on vacation—and get them on the phone in time for your deadline.

Once you've achieved some results using PR persons, they can also serve as sort of an executive tranquilizer. Often, PR staffers will want to sit in on interviews with their bosses. The PR person can provide a little comfort zone for your source who believes (usually wrongly) that their PR person will stop them if they say something wrong. As a result, they may be a little freer with their conversation. The PR person can also help translate their jargon, remind them of information they have forgotten and make notes for a follow-up if the source can't remember something important, saving embarrassment all around.

Should you worry about the PR staffer taking notes? No: It should work to your advantage. Assuming you do your work right and quote the source accurately, those notes are your protection. If the source has said something he or she regrets and complains about "misquotes," you can have the pleasure of referring the source back to his own PR department. That's always fun.

And, if the interview is a dud, you can always use the PR department as a place to which you can complain—or ask for a new source.

The PR department can be helpful for follow-up information, since it is likely that they have learned something new as a result of the experience. A PR person should be able to get follow-up questions answered to fill in factoids without a time-wasting second interview. When I was on the job at the Archdiocese, I became an expert on church-finance issues, the liturgical calendar and Catholic School Board meeting schedules. I could provide names, dates and numbers to writers without delay.

In conclusion, here's my advice on working successfully with PR departments. First, be willing to play a little of the game and treat the PR staff as people. Be honest about your needs. Be fair in what you expect from them. Be firm in getting access. Develop a civil and, if possible, friendly relationship.

Second, use the expertise of the PR department in understanding their own company or institution, not your special interest. They probably can't answer your questions, but they probably know who can. And they probably can help you find that Dr. Livingston in their institutional jungle.

Third, give the PR department feedback on the sources they provide. If the source was awful and you didn't get what you need, let them know. Maybe they can get someone else or maybe not, but they can keep that source out of the loop in the future and not waste your time.

Can you ever expect a PR person to give you some *real* news? Probably not. On the other hand, Deep Throat came from somewhere—maybe even the PR department.

# Publicists Are Writers' Allies

*By Michele Kelly*

I opened the *Chicago Tribune* and there it was again. A columnist had written that "publicists are the nearest thing to bald-faced liars." Yet another endearing reference to my profession.

Surely, public relations and journalism both are guilty of having unscrupulous members. How about setting up interviews with journalists who don't show up? Or the reporters who demonstrate proficiency with colorful, abusive language over the phone? Or, best yet, the ones who tell you you're blacklisted because your client was not available for an interview at a certain time? Fortunately, these types are greatly outnumbered by writers who are pleasant, professional and highly competent.

If a publicist believes in the profession's code of ethics and understands the job at hand, they view writers: (1) as influential people who present all sides of an issue, (2) as very, very busy people, and (3) as partners.

Thus, it is with the utmost respect, integrity and business acumen that we approach writers. If you are treated with anything less, then it isn't a "public relations" issue, it's a "people" issue.

So, lay aside the labels and take advantage of those who can help connect you with useful information and people, while saving you time and money. A publicist can be a researcher, a secretary, a photographer and an interpreter available to work with you on virtually every story you write—at no cost to you.

The right publicist can be found in O'Dwyer's Directory of Public Relations Firms, which is updated yearly. This book, which can be found at many libraries, lists public relations firms according to specific industries such as health, sports and finance. It also lists key clients of many firms.

Check out *Crain's Chicago Business'* biannual top 25 list of PR firms. They're ranked by fee income, so these firms are the heavy hitters with "name" clients.

The final way to locate the PR sources who will be of greatest help is by word of mouth. Ask writers and publicists you know. You may think the latter group would be close-mouthed about sharing competitor names, but that is simply not true. When a writer needs a specific interview or information, and we know another firm can help, we pass along a name and number. It's part of a publicist's ongoing goal to help the media find what and whom they're looking for.

The wide range of assistance a publicist can provide was recently demonstrated when a reporter from the *Daily Herald* showed interest in folk musician Lee Murdock, a client of my firm, LoDestro Public Relations. Spanning five months, we invested more than 35 hours in assisting the reporter who, by the way, treated us like a true partner, not an adversary. In that time, we prepared a list of more than 30 supporting interview candidates from varying geographic locations that coincided with the paper's readership areas.

We helped arrange a photo shoot in the recording studio that captured Lee in a way unique to that story. We prepared written material on Lee's new album, provided an itinerary of his schedule and researched specific questions about the folk-music industry. Above all, we didn't pester the reporter.

There are lots of ways to maximize your own relationship with publicists. In brainstorming the following suggestions, I turned to my PR counterpart in Chicago, Kathy Posner, vice president of COMM2. Both our firms hold to a philosophy that the media are our associates and that we are here to meet their requirements by providing information, showing all sides of an issue, educating them on unfamiliar subjects and arranging access to leaders in a given field.

Incorporating even half of the following suggestions can produce quicker results and a more pleasant experience when working with publicists.

## WHAT TO EXPECT FROM A PUBLICIST

■ A publicist should give writers not only information on their own particular client, but also background information on whatever industry the client is involved in.

■ A publicist should provide names or information on competitors so the writer has a broad range of information.

■ A publicist should be treated as a "librarian" who can do research for a writer. Many of us collect extensive material on our client's or company's industry. If material is not readily available, ask that they find it for you.

■ Many more writers today are addressing technological issues in many areas of business and life. Require the publicist to double-check technical terms, spellings and references.

■ A writer should never expect "freebies," but, when offered, accept them graciously as long as they are not in conflict with any policy of the media that the writer represents.

## HOW TO GET MORE FROM A PUBLICIST

■ Tell publicists which days and times are best for reaching you. This will avoid an overweight message bin or calls while you're on deadline.

- Writers need to be specific about deadlines. Tell publicists when you need to confirm an interview time and date. Give as much lead time as possible. By setting a deadline for a confirmation, you can line up another interview. A good publicist will offer alternative suggestions.

- At Fortune 500 companies, communications departments screen most journalists' requests. To speed this process, write some basic questions in a "Request for Information" memo, fax it to the department and designate a specific deadline for an interview. Follow up with a phone call. This can expedite the interview and save you from the grand game of phone tag.

- If you're interested in an upcoming speech that you cannot attend, request a cassette tape, a transcript or an advance copy of the speech.

- All media (especially freelancers who may need photographs to complement a story) should ask the publicist to arrange and/or provide them. There are a lot of visual opportunities that a company's photographer can provide if given guidance from an editor or writer.

Writers should realize that the publicist exists to serve a writer's needs, not the publicist's needs. While PR people call writers all the time to pitch stories on their clients, writers can call publicists when an expert source or background information is needed for a story.

Forming friendships or close working relationships with publicists can help writers better understand how publicists can help them. If a writer is interested in "scoops" in a particular subject area and a publicist is comfortable and trusts that writer, the publicist is much more likely to provide information on breaking stories. You can even request home phone numbers of the publicist and key spokespersons.

Be aware that professional public relations counselors don't view media coverage as a favor, but as a collaborative effort to inform people. And that's why a publicist could be a most important ally for every writer.

# Trade Magazines
## An Editor Discusses Writing for Trade Publications

*By Jerry DeMuth*

The Chicago area is home to more than 100 trade magazines, many published by such major trade-oriented companies as Cahners Publishing Co., Communication Channels Inc., Crain Communications Inc., Faulkner & Gray and MacLean Hunter Publishing Co. Numerous trade associations produce dozens of others. These periodicals can broaden opportunities, but often writers are either unaware of all but the few on newsstands do not know how to enter this market or if it is worth entering.

NWU asked Al Girardi to draw on his experiences and provide advice and insight for those interested in marketing their writing to trade publications. Girardi is presently the editor of Communication Channel's Midwest Real Estate News. Before entering the trade field, he was managing editor of *New Heritage,* an East Coast arts and cultural-affairs magazine. He also has written for the Associated Press and newspapers in Mississippi, Alabama and Long Island.

**NWU: How can writers interested in writing for a certain trade discover what magazines serve that trade?**

Girardi: Go to the library and look in Standard Rate & Data. Sometimes it's difficult to tell from the name exactly what the publication is about, but usually it's a good indication. Like Midwest Real Estate News: The title doesn't tell you it's about commercial real estate, but it does tell you it's a real estate book. Swine Practitioner tells you it's a book for pig doctors. Or you can find a pro in the field and ask him what he reads. If you want to get into the banking field, find out what a banker reads. Also, a trade association should know and they might even have a library. Often trade associations have their own magazines.

After you do this preliminary work, and before you send a query letter, call up the magazine and find out exactly what they cover. Maybe talk to a secretary before you talk to an editor. For instance, if you send me a query letter or an article on residential real estate, it's going to influence me in a negative way. I'll say you don't know my magazine or industry enough to write for me. Knowing the book shows initiative and a certain level of journalistic skill, and impressing somebody with your professionalism are keys to getting an assignment.

**NWU: How can you break into the trade-magazine market?**

Girardi: Clips are the most important thing. When I need someone to write a certain story I'm really hoping to get someone who knows what they're doing. The impact on my production schedule is too serious if I assign a story, and the writer screws it up. If someone has done only a few things for a community newspaper, I can't take a chance and assign a story to that writer.

There's a kind of hierarchy of situations. Do you go with someone who knows real estate but maybe isn't the best bang-up writer in the world, or do you go with someone who's a good writer but can't show you clips in your own specialty? It depends on what I see in the clips I'm shown. If it's a banking clip and the subject is complex and the writer shows a good grasp of it, plus I sense a certain adaptability—there's a retail clip, a report on the stock market, maybe a PR clip and a brochure—then I may go with that writer.

This is what a good journalist is all about. A good journalist should be able to walk into a situation, grasp what's going on, and be able to report on that subject no matter what it is. It's not so much what you know—although that helps—it's what you know about getting information.

So I would prefer to go with a skilled journalist than someone who knows my field but doesn't write really well.

**NWU: How can a writer, who is good but lacks experience in the field, break into a trade magazine?**

Girardi: The best way to get to the editor is to go out and write a story. First you have to pick up the book and look at its style. In our book we have city area reviews. If someone comes to me and can pick a city and show me he can write a good city review in our format, how can I object if it's a good story?

**NWU: Is covering a trade show a good way to break in?**

Girardi: Sometimes. But it could also get you in the waste can if it's not on target. To find out what you should cover, talk it over with the editor. Or ask if there's anything in particular the editor wants you to write about.

**NWU: Will a writer be left on his or her own, or can a writer expect some help from an editor when putting together an article? Will the editor help provide focus or an angle?**

Girardi: The editor can be a resource. If you say to him, "What's your sense of the way things are going? What's hot?," he can help you not repeat what's been said and write an article that's more interesting and will grab attention.

**NWU: How open to freelancers are trade magazines?**

Girardi: Trade association magazines tend to have in-house people do the writing. But most trade magazines use freelancers. However, some don't pay. They don't have to because they can get people within their trade to write for practically nothing. Then you have the PR machines pumping out pulp and you have books that run it. For some magazines it's not that important to get a good writer involved because they just want to fill up space.

A lot of trade mags have cut their staffs. In a way, that has meant more work for freelancers. But more editors are turning to amateurs and also to PR. Shorter, newsier pieces usually will be staff written. You don't need a freelancer to write a news blurb. All of our departments—which are the shorter, newsier types of things—are staff written.

As a general rule, if it's going to cost more money for a magazine to cover it than to get a freelancer to do it, they probably will use a freelancer.

**NWU: How much can a writer expect from a trade magazine that does pay?**

Girardi: Many trade magazines pay about 10 cents a word, which isn't a lot of money. Fifteen cents a word is better, 20 cents is what I pay.

If you have a good relationship with an editor, it helps because there's a sense of rapport. I know I can count on certain writers to write what I need, and I'll go out of my way to throw in another $25, sometimes $50, their way.

We pay a flat rate [i.e., expenses are not paid] and with one writer who had extra phone costs I threw in another $25 for each story for the next two months. Maintaining that relationship was important.

If you have an editor who can be trusted and you can build a relationship with that editor by doing extra things, you have a steady source of income and you have someone who is likely to bend the rules a little bit when you need it.

**NWU: Do trade editors spell out what they want or expect, or what they will pay?**

Girardi: I always say, "Get it in writing!" I always send out a very clear letter detailing how much, when, where and how many words. And some suggestions, some recommendations, some requirements. That's it.

Finding out how much a trade magazine pays is a hard thing. It would be nice if you could call up and find out. But usually you don't find out until you're in the middle of negotiations.

**NWU: Do trade magazines serving prestigious or monied fields pay more than magazines serving grittier fields?**

Girardi: A prestigious field is no indication of what kind of money they pay.

**NWU: What about selling the same or a similar article to another publication to get more income from your work?**

Girardi: If it's the same story, forget it—then it becomes one of those canned stories the PR agencies send out. That would also destroy your relationship with an editor. It's really stupid to think in the short-term about getting a couple extra bucks for the same article and annihilate your ties to a magazine.

But if you can alter a story significantly, then the editor is not going to have a lot of trouble with your using the same information, or even some of the same sentences. If it's in a magazine in a different field, I'll demand less of an alteration than if it's in a competing magazine.

Reworking it means more than just changing the lead and keeping the rest of it the same. You don't have to change every word, but you should try to create something that's somewhat different. Maybe not redo it, but rework it.

**NWU: Any advice you can give that a writer should always follow?**

Girardi: A writer should always provide more information than the bare necessity and have the editor cut. If you're assigned an article of 2,500 words, don't turn in 2,400 words. If you give the editor a little less than assigned and he happens to be in trouble for space that issue, he's going to remember and not use you again. Cover a little bit more, get a little more detail, turn in 2,600 or 2,800 words. An editor will appreciate that and keep you in mind in the future.

# By PUBLICATION

## What Publishers Expect from Writers

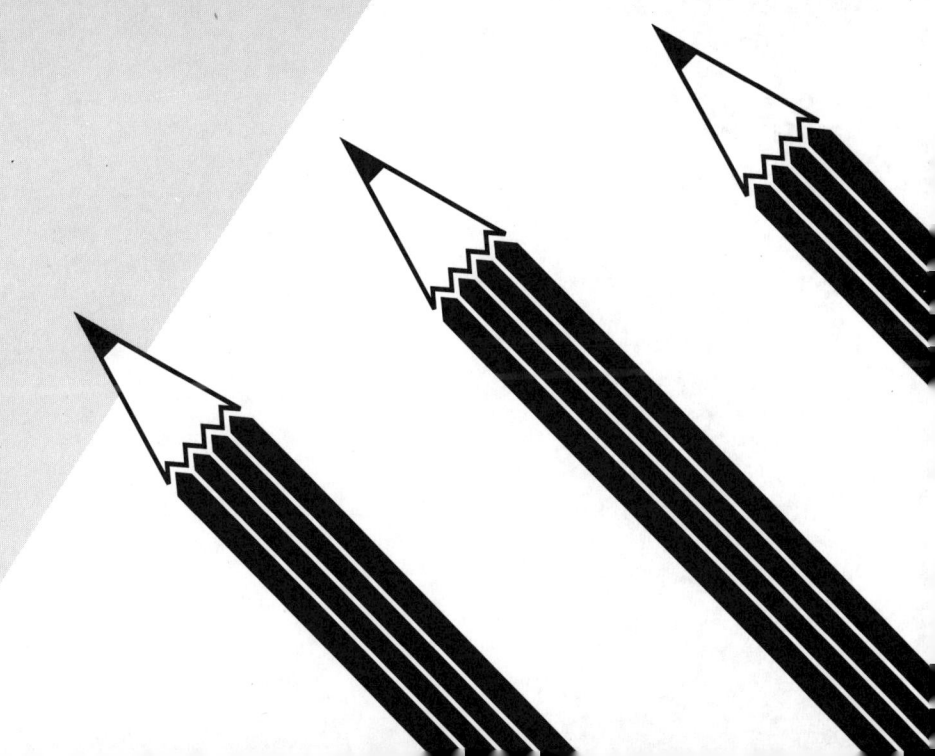

# Magazines

**ABA Journal**

*Association Monthly*

The Lawyer's Magazine
750 N. Lake Shore Drive
Chicago, IL 60611
312-988-5000

---

**Payment Information**

Advance paid .................. None      Kill Fee .................. Neg.

Expenses paid

........Y.......... Travel              ........Y.......... Fax

........Y.......... Overnight Del.      ........Y.......Phone

---

Payment is 100% on acceptance. No payment for rewrites or updates. Survey respondent doesn't indicate payment for syndication, reprints or resales.

### Submission Criteria And Policy

ABA Journal considers unsolicited manuscripts, and reviews queries in 2 to 4 weeks. They use a written contract, and acquire First North American Serial rights.

ABA Journal accepts simultaneous submissions and proposals for articles over the telephone.

### Publication Buys Freelance Submissions On...

| Category | Min. Words | Max. Words | Min. Pay. | Max. Pay. | Per | Cont. |
|---|---|---|---|---|---|---|
| News | 250 | 750 | $150.00 | $250.00 | Story | D. Moss |
| Feature Stories | 3000 | 3500 | | $3000.00 | Story | B. Yates |

**Advice for Writers:** Read the publication.

### Editorial Comments:

Although the survey respondent indicated that the rights bought are First North American Serial, the contract stipulates "work for hire." The contract does not contain a clause stipulating payment.

# Magazines

**Access**
*Association Monthly*

American Dental Hygienists' Assn.
444 N. Michigan Ave., #3400
Chicago, IL 60611
312-440-8929

---
**Payment Information**

Advance paid .................. None     Kill Fee .................. None

Expenses paid

........N.......... Travel          ........N.......... Fax

........N.......... Overnight Del.  ........N...... Phone

---

Payment is 100% on submission, and an unspecified amount for updates. No payment for rewrites, syndication, reprints or resales.

### Submission Criteria And Policy

Access considers unsolicited manuscripts, and accepts or rejects an assignment in 2 weeks. They use a written contract; see Comments for rights information.

Access does not accept simultaneous submissions. They accept proposals for articles over the telephone.

They ask writers to provide photographs, yet offer no payment.

### Publication Buys Freelance Submissions On...

| Category | Min. Words | Max. Words | Min. Pay. | Max. Pay. | Per | Cont. |
|---|---|---|---|---|---|---|
| Clinical/Scientific | | | | | | J. Majeski |
| Feature Stories | 1000 | 4000 | $300.00 | $500.00 | Story | S. Lyons |
| Shorts | 500 | 500 | $100.00 | $100.00 | Story | S. Lyons |

# Magazines

**Advice for Writers**
Call first or write and send samples.

**Editorial Comments:**
The copyright in the agreement appears to cover all rights, including rights to all working papers and notes. It takes approximately one month to review a manuscript. No rate was specified for clinical/scientific articles.

# Magazines

## Advertising Age
Weekly Trade Journal

Crain Communications
740 N. Rush
Chicago, IL 60611
312-649-5320

### Payment Information

Advance paid ................... None    Kill Fee ................... Neg.

Expenses paid

........Y.......... Travel           ........Y......... Fax

........Y.......... Overnight Del.   ........Y..... Phone

Payment is 100% on publication, but no payment for rewrites, updates, syndication, reprints or resales.

### Submission Criteria And Policy

Advertising Age does not consider unsolicited manuscripts, and accepts or rejects an assignment in 2 to 4 weeks. They use both written and verbal contracts and acquire all rights.

Advertising Age does not accept simultaneous submissions. They accept proposals for articles over the telephone.

They ask writers to provide photographs; payment varies.

### Publication Buys Freelance Submissions On...

| Category | Min. Words | Max. Words | Min. Pay. | Max. Pay. | Per | Cont. |
|---|---|---|---|---|---|---|
| Forum Essay | 400 | 800 | $100.00 | $350.00 | Story | |
| Feature Stories | 1000 | 2000 | $350.00 | $1000.00 | Story | |

44

# Magazines

**Advice for Writers:**
"Don't count on us—we accept very little, but you might hit it right if you study the publication and search for news."

**Editorial Comments:**
They answered both yes and no to the question about paying for an update. The kill fee is a flat fee; amounts vary.

# Magazines

## Barrister Magazine

Association Quarterly for
Young Lawyers

ABA Press
750 N. Lake Shore Drive
Chicago, IL 60611
312-988-6047

---

**Payment Information**

Advance paid .................. None          Kill Fee .. See Comments

Expenses paid

........N......... Travel              .........Y......... Fax

.........Y.......... Overnight Del.    .........Y..... Phone

---

There is no payment for book reviews or opinion pieces ("by young lawyers—no payment"); survey respondent didn't specify when writers could expect payment for feature stories. Payment for rewrites and updates (see Comments). No payment for syndication, reprints or resales.

### Submission Criteria And Policy

Barrister considers unsolicited manuscripts, and accepts or rejects an assignment in 2 to 4 weeks. They use a written contract and acquire one-time rights.

Barrister does not accept simultaneous submissions. "We prefer to be the publisher of choice." They do not accept proposals for articles over the telephone.

They ask writers to provide photographs. Payment is $75-$100 on publication."

### Publication Buys Freelance Submissions On...

| Category | Min. Words | Max. Words | Min. Pay. | Max. Pay. | Per | Cont. |
|---|---|---|---|---|---|---|
| Book Reviews | 750 | | | | Story | V. Quade |
| Feature Stories | 1000 | 2500 | $250.00 | $1000.00 | Story | V. Quade |
| Opinion Pieces | | | | | | V. Quade |

46

# Magazines

**Advice for Writers:**
"Think of articles that pertain directly to young lawyers."

**Editorial Comments:**
For kill fee, the survey respondent wrote, "If assignment is fulfilled but we decide not to use it, kill fee is 100% of contract. I don't believe in percentage kill fees." They pay for rewrites "if assignment has changed" and for updates "if delay is caused by us." They buy one-time rights, but the contract is for contribution to a collective work and calls for "exclusive right of first publication...throughout the world as part of the publication named above" and non-exclusive right to reprint and license "in any medium or form of communication in the English language, to others" and to use it "or any part thereof, in any other publication produced by the ABA."

# Magazines

## Campus Life

Monthly Consumer Magazine

Christianity Today
465 Gundersen Drive
Carol Stream, IL 60188
708-260-6200

---

**Payment Information**

Advance paid .................. None        Kill Fee .................. 50%

Expenses paid

........Y......... Travel              ........N......... Fax

........N......... Overnight Del.      ........Y...... Phone

---

Payment is 100% on acceptance. No payment for rewrites, syndication or resales; $50 payment for reprints.

### Submission Criteria And Policy

Campus Life does not consider unsolicited manuscripts, and accepts or rejects an assignment in 3 to 5 weeks. They use a written contract, and acquire First North American Serial rights.

Campus Life accepts simultaneous submissions. They do not accept proposals for articles over the telephone.

### Publication Buys Freelance Submissions On...

| Category | Min. Words | Max. Words | Min. Pay. | Max. Pay. | Per | Cont. |
|---|---|---|---|---|---|---|
| First Person Prof. | 750 | 2500 | $.10 | $.20 | Word | |
| Feature Stories | 500 | 2500 | $.10 | $.20 | Word | |
| Anecdotal Comm. | 500 | 750 | $.10 | $.20 | Word | |

### Advice for Writers:

"Submit as-told-to first-person stories about teen everyday experiences."

# Magazines

**Editorial Comments:**
"While not overtly religious, Campus Life is a magazine with a Christian perspective on life. Writers must have sensitivity and empathy toward this perspective." Survey respondent indicates they pay 27.5¢ per mile travel as an advance, but may have misunderstood the advance part of the question. The most frequently covered topics are "teen concerns: friendship, sex and dating, self-concept." Sample copies are available for $2 plus SASE.

# Magazines

**Catalyst**

*Bimonthly on School Reform*

Voices of Chicago School Reform
332 S. Michigan Avenue
Chicago, Illinois 60604
312-427-4830

---

**Payment Information**

Advance paid .................. None        Kill Fee .................. 20%

Expenses paid

........Y........ Travel              .......N........ Fax

........N........ Overnight Del.      .......Y...... Phone

---

Payment is 100% on acceptance. No payment for rewrites, syndication, reprints or resales, but they do pay for updates. They pay for parking, long-distance phone calls and purchase of publications for research, if approved in advance.

**Submission Criteria And Policy**

Catalyst does not consider unsolicited manuscripts, and "works with writers until a piece is acceptable." They use a written contract, and acquire various rights.

They do not accept proposals for articles over the telephone or simultaneous submissions.

**Publication Buys Freelance Submissions On...**

| Category | Min. Words | Max. Words | Min. Pay. | Max. Pay. | Per | Cont. |
|---|---|---|---|---|---|---|
| News | 300 | 2400 | $100.00 | $1500.00 | Story | L. Lenz |
| Feature Stories | 300 | 2400 | $100.00 | $1500.00 | Story | L. Lenz |
| Departmental | 300 | 1800 | $100.00 | $800.00 | Story | L. Lenz |

**Advice for Writers:**
"Knowledge of education helps immensely; be on time; use floppy disks in Wordperfect or ASCII, IBM compatible; AP Style."

# Magazines

**Editorial Comments:**
Stories are by assignment. "We look for regular freelancers who will develop knowledge here on Chicago public schools and education in general. They consider the kill fee "a formality—we've never killed an assigned story."

# Magazines

**Chicago**

Monthly Consumer Magazine

414 N. Orleans Ave., #800
Chicago, IL 60610
312-222-8999

---

**Payment Information**

Advance paid ................... None    Kill Fee ................. 25%

Expenses paid

.........Y......... Travel           .......Y........ Fax

.........Y......... Overnight Del.   .......Y....... Phone

---

Payment is 100% on acceptance. No payment for rewrites or updates. They purchase First North American Serial rights.

**Submission Criteria And Policy**

Chicago rarely considers unsolicited manuscripts. They review queries within a few weeks and they do the first edit of a manuscript within a few weeks.

Chicago frowns on simultaneous submissions, and they do not accept proposals for articles over the telephone.

**Publication Buys Freelance Submissions On...**

| Category | Min. Words | Max. Words | Min. Pay. | Max. Pay. | Per | Cont. |
|---|---|---|---|---|---|---|
| Frontlines | 100 | 300 | $100.00 | $300.00 | Story | D. Santow |
| Feature Stories | 2000 | 4000 | $2000.00 | $4000.00 | Story | R. Babcock |
| Columns | 850 | 1500 | $700.00 | $1000.00 | Story | R. Babcock |

**Editorial Comments:**

At $1 a word, Chicago is the best-paying, mass-media periodical in the Midwest. But beware of the 25% kill fee.

# Magazines

**Advice for Writers:**
We received this information from an insider: "If you're trying to break in, try writing a few Frontlines pieces first. The monthly columns are usually written by the same people each month, so this is not a good market for freelancers. A freelancer is more likely to get a big feature if he or she has already had some Frontlines items published."

# Magazines

**Chicago Enterprise**

*Monthly with Economic Focus*

Commercial Club of Chicago
One First National Plaza
#2700
Chicago, IL 60603
312-853-1203

| Payment Information |  |
|---|---|
| Advance paid .................. None | Kill Fee ................... 33% |
| Expenses paid | |
| ........Y......... Travel | .......Y........ Fax |
| ........Y......... Overnight Del. | .......Y....... Phone |

Payment is 100% on acceptance. No payment for rewrites, syndication, reprints or resales. They do pay for updates.

### Submission Criteria And Policy

Chicago Enterprise considers unsolicited manuscripts, and accepts or rejects an assignment in 3 to 6 weeks. They use a written contract, and acquire one-time rights.

Chicago Enterprise accepts simultaneous submissions. They accept proposals for articles over the telephone, "but a query will be requested."

### Publication Buys Freelance Submissions On...

| Category | Min. Words | Max. Words | Min. Pay. | Max. Pay. | Per | Cont. |
|---|---|---|---|---|---|---|
| Departmental | 900 | 1200 | | $500.00 | Story | |
| Feature Stories | | 1200 | | $500.00 | Story | |
| Book Reviews | | 1000 | | $150.00 | Story | |

### Advice for Writers:

"Our standards for writing and reporting are high. Know the Chicago area and shun clichéd ideas. No 'how-to' articles or technical pieces."

# Magazines

**Editorial Comments:**
Some terms from their contract: payment within 30 days of acceptance, rights reverting to writer 90 days after date of publication. The editor indicates the magazine covers "Chicago area economic development." "We will work with writers new to our magazine if they pose good ideas and offer evidence of their ability to execute them."

# Magazines

## Chicago Life Magazine
*Consumer Magazine*

P.O. Box 11311
Chicago, IL 60611
312-528-2737

### Payment Information

| | |
|---|---|
| Advance paid .................. None | Kill Fee ................ None |

Expenses paid

| | |
|---|---|
| .........N......... Travel | ........N...... Fax |
| .........N......... Overnight Del. | ........N...... Phone |

Payment is 100% on publication. No payment for rewrites, updates, syndication, reprints or resales.

### Submission Criteria And Policy

Chicago Life Magazine considers unsolicited manuscripts, and accepts or rejects an assignment in 2 weeks if accompanied by SASE. They do not use a contract, and acquire one-time rights.

Chicago Life Magazine sometimes accepts simultaneous submissions, depending on the market. They do not accept proposals for articles over the telephone.

### Publication Buys Freelance Submissions On...

| Category | Min. Words | Max. Words | Min. Pay. | Max. Pay. | Per | Cont. |
|---|---|---|---|---|---|---|
| News | 500 | 2000 | $15.00 | $30.00 | Story | P. Lyon |
| Feature Stories | 500 | 2000 | $15.00 | $30.00 | Story | P. Lyon |
| Reviews | 500 | 2000 | $15.00 | $30.00 | Story | P. Lyon |
| Opinion Pieces | 500 | 2000 | $15.00 | $30.00 | Story | P. Lyon |

### Advice for Writers:

"Any submissions should be as tight, concise and as specific as possible. Meet all deadlines."

# Magazines

**Editorial Comments:**
The topics most frequently covered are: "health, fitness, finance, travel, politics." While they sometimes accept simultaneous submissions, they don't assign articles. They sometimes ask writers to provide photographs and payment "depends." Free sample copies are available by sending a self-addressed 9" x 12" envelope with seven stamps on it.

# Magazines

## Chicago Nightlines
*Weekly Magazine*

3059 N. Southport
Chicago, IL 60657
312-871-7610

### Payment Information

Advance paid .................. None          Kill Fee ...See Comments

Expenses paid

.................. Travel                    .................. Fax

.................. Overnight Del.            .............. Phone

Payment is 100%, 4 to 6 weeks after publication. No payment for rewrites, syndication, reprints or resales, but they do pay for updates.

### Submission Criteria And Policy

Chicago Outlines considers unsolicited manuscripts, and accepts or rejects an assignment in 2 to 5 weeks. They use a verbal contract, and acquire one-time rights.

Chicago Outlines accepts simultaneous submissions. They accept proposals for articles over the telephone, "primarily from established contacts."

### Publication Buys Freelance Submissions On...

| Category | Min. Words | Max. Words | Min. Pay. | Max. Pay. | Per | Cont. |
|---|---|---|---|---|---|---|
| Reviews | 200 | 450 | $15.00 | | Story | T. Baim |
| Feature Stories | 750 | 2000 | $25.00 | $35.00 | Story | T. Baim |
| Opinion Pieces | 500 | 700 | $20.00 | $25.00 | Story | T. Baim |
| Departmental | 300 | 1000 | $15.00 | $35.00 | Story | T. Baim |
| News | 300 | 750 | $15.00 | $25.00 | Story | T. Baim |

# Magazines

**Editorial Comments:**
"Establish ability to freelance and [define] areas of interest before submission. Be aggressive with fresh ideas and understand publishers and editors of small publications are very busy and may take a while to get back to you—don't take it personally and don't give up easy. We use the Associated Press Style Manual for the majority of proofreading issues." They pay $5-$10 for photos, depending on the story. They will not pay for photos supplied by a publicity department.

# Magazines

## Chicago Parent News
Monthly News Magazine

141 S. Oak Park Ave.
Oak Park, IL 60302
708-386-5555

---

**Payment Information**

Advance paid .................. None     Kill Fee .................. 100%

Expenses paid
..........Y........ Travel              .........N........ Fax
..........N........ Overnight Del.      .........N..... Phone

---

Payment is 100% on publication. No payment for rewrites; "sometimes" pay for updates. They don't indicate payment for syndication, reprints or resales.

### Submission Criteria And Policy

They use a verbal contract and acquire one-time rights.

Chicago Parent accepts simultaneous submissions. They prefer queries to proposals for articles over the telephone.

### Publication Buys Freelance Submissions On...

| Category | Min. Words | Max. Words | Min. Pay. | Max. Pay. | Per | Cont. |
|---|---|---|---|---|---|---|
| Feature Stories | 1200 | 2000 | $100.00 | $200.00 | Story | M. Haley |

### Advice for Writers:
"Prefer copy on spec from writers who are new to us."

# Newspapers

## Chicago Reader
Weekly Newspaper

11 E. Illinois Street
Chicago, IL 60611
312-828-0350

---

**Payment Information**

Advance paid .................. None     Kill Fee ................. None

Expenses paid

.........N......... Travel          .......N....... Fax

.........N......... Overnight Del.  .......N..... Phone

---

Payment is 100% on publication. No payment for rewrites, updates, syndication, reprints or resales.

### Submission Criteria And Policy

Chicago Reader considers unsolicited manuscripts, and accepts or rejects an assignment in 3 to 24 weeks. They do not use a contract, and acquire First North American Serial rights.

Chicago Reader accepts simultaneous submissions. They accept proposals for articles over the telephone.

### Publication Buys Freelance Submissions On...

| Category | Min. Words | Max. Words | Min. Pay. | Max. Pay. | Per | Cont. |
|---|---|---|---|---|---|---|
| News | 1500 | | $210.00 | $1400.00 | Story | A. True |
| Feature Stories | 3000 | | $200.00 | $1400.00 | Story | A. True |
| Opinion Pieces | 1500 | 4000 | | $210 | Story | A. True |
| Book Reviews | 1500 | 4000 | | $210 | Story | L. Molzahn |
| Theatre Reviews | 750 | 1500 | | $110.00 | Story | L. Molzahn |
| Film Reviews | 1000 | 4000 | $140.00 | $160.00 | Story | L. Molzahn |
| Music Reviews | 1000 | 4000 | $110.00 | $210.00 | Story | A. True |

### Advice for Writers:
"Read the paper and try to imagine where and how your story fits in before calling. Have a story in mind, not just a subject. Keep it local."

# Newspapers

## Chicago Reporter
*Monthly Publication on Social Issues*

332 S. Michigan Avenue, #500
Chicago, IL 60604
312-427-4830

---

**Payment Information**

Advance paid .................. Flat Amt.    Kill Fee .......... $100-$200

Expenses paid

.......... N ........ Travel           ....... N .......... Fax

.......... N ........ Overnight Del.   ....... N ....... Phone

---

Payment is 100% on acceptance. No payment for rewrites, but they do pay for updates. Syndication, reprints and resales don't apply.

### Submission Criteria And Policy

Chicago Reporter does not consider unsolicited manuscripts, and accepts or rejects an assignment in 1 to 4 weeks. They use a written contract, and acquire one-time rights.

Chicago Reporter does not accept simultaneous submissions. "We want exclusivity of an idea as well as a story." They accept proposals for articles over the telephone for "original pitch, then a written follow-up."

### Publication Buys Freelance Submissions On...

| Category | Min. Words | Max. Words | Min. Pay. | Max. Pay. | Per | Cont. |
|---|---|---|---|---|---|---|
| News | 1000 | 3000 | $250.00 | $1000.00 | Story | L. Washington |

### Advice for Writers:
"Be specific with idea and content of story. Avoid being cosmic."

### Editorial Comments:
They pay for cabs and parking.

# Newspapers

## Chicago Tribune
*Daily Newspaper*

435 N. Michigan Ave.
Chicago, IL 60611
312-222-3232

---

**Payment Information**

Advance paid .................. None      Kill Fee .................. Var.

Expenses paid

........N......... Travel           ........N......... Fax

........N........ Overnight Del.    ........N...... Phone

---

Payment is 100% on acceptance, but freelancers complain that payment is often held up for weeks and requires follow-up calls. No payment for rewrites, updates, syndication, reprints or resales.

### Submission Criteria And Policy

Chicago Tribune considers unsolicited manuscripts, and accepts or rejects an assignment in 3 to 4 weeks. They use a verbal contract and acquire various rights.

The Tribune accepts simultaneous submissions "as long as it isn't in another Chicago paper." They accept proposals for articles over the telephone.

### Publication Buys Freelance Submissions On...

| Category | Min. Words | Max. Words | Min. Pay. | Max. Pay. | Per | Cont. |
|---|---|---|---|---|---|---|
| Sunday Magazine | 1500 | 3000 | $500.00 | $15000.00 | Story | Editor |
| Daily Features | 400 | 2000 | $100.00 | $350.00 | Story | Editor |
| Chicago Tempo | 700 | 3000 | $150.00 | $350.00 | Story | Editor |
| Suburban Tempo | 100 | 2000 | $20.00 | $325.00 | Story | S. Lough |

# Newspapers

**Advice for Writers:**
The Home editor advises, "Know our section. You'd be surprised how many submissions have to do with real estate or do-it-yourself projects." Additional sections accepting freelance articles include Tempo, WomaNews, Travel, Arts and the Opinion pages. Query the appropriate editor.

**Editorial Comments:**
For stories involving long-distance calls, you may be able to go to a Trib office and use their phones. Although the editors accept story proposals over the phone, they strongly prefer written queries.

# Magazines

**Christian Century**
*Ecumenical Weekly*

407 S. Dearborn
Chicago, IL 60605
312-427-5380

### Payment Information

Advance paid ................ None    Kill Fee ................None

Expenses paid
   .........N....... Travel       .......N........ Fax
   .........N........ Overnight Del.    .......N...... Phone

Payment is 100% on publication. No payment for rewrites, updates, syndication, reprints or resales.

### Submission Criteria And Policy

Christian Century considers unsolicited manuscripts, and accepts or rejects an assignment in 2 to 4 weeks. They do not use a contract, and acquire all rights.

Christian Century does not accept simultaneous submissions. They do not accept proposals for articles over the telephone.

### Publication Buys Freelance Submissions On...

| Category | Min. Words | Max. Words | Min. Pay. | Max. Pay. | Per | Cont. |
|---|---|---|---|---|---|---|
| Opinion Pieces | 1000 | 1500 | $75.00 | | Story | Mng. Editor |
| Feature Stories | 2000 | 3000 | $125.00 | | Story | Mng. Editor |

### Advice for Writers:

"Must be very familiar with audience for our magazine—theologically sophisticated, socially engaged."

# Magazines

## Christianity Today
*Non-Denominational Monthly*

465 Gundersen Dr.
Carol Stream, IL 60188
708-260-6200

### Payment Information

Advance paid .................. None      Kill Fee ................Rarely

Expenses paid

..........Y.......... Travel           ........Y........ Fax

..........Y.......... Overnight Del.   ........Y...... Phone

All expenses are negotiable. Payment is 4 weeks before publication. They generally do not pay for rewrites but do pay for updates, "if we hold onto story and article was out of date." Regarding syndication, reprints or resales, "we refer requests to authors in most cases, except for small circulation foreign publications which we sometimes give our articles to, without charge."

### Submission Criteria And Policy

Christianity Today accepts or rejects an assignment within 2 to 4 weeks. They have no contract and rights vary.

They prefer single submissions. Sometimes they ask writers for photos for news stories if photographs are decent. Payment is negotiable.

### Publication Buys Freelance Submissions On...

| Category | Min.. Words | Max. Words | Min. Pay. | Max. Pay. | Per | Cont. |
|---|---|---|---|---|---|---|
| News | 250 | 2000 | $.09 | $.10 | Word | |
| Feature Stories | 1000 | 3000 | $.09 | $.10 | Word | |
| Book Reviews | 750 | 850 | $.09 | $.10 | Word | |
| Opinion Pieces | 500 | | $.09 | $.10 | Word | |
| Essays | 1500 | 4000 | $.09 | $.10 | Word | |

# Magazines

**Advice for Writers:**
"Query first. We prefer written queries for most articles. For extremely timely news articles, telephone our news department."

**Editorial Comments:**
Christianity Today reserves the right to anthologize articles. "Most of our work is done with people we have a track record with, often by phone. We will work with first-time writers on spec." Most rates of pay quoted above apply to first-time writers. The magazine is pubished 15 times per year.

# Newspapers

## City & State
*Monthly Newspaper*

Crain Communications
740 N. Rush St., 2nd Floor
Chicago, IL 60611
312-649-5200

---

**Payment Information**

Advance paid ................... None       Kill Fee .................. $50

Expenses paid

........Y.......... Travel              ........Y........ Fax

........Y.......... Overnight Del.      ........Y...... Phone

---

Payment is 100% on acceptance. No payment for rewrites, syndication, reprints or resales, but they pay "same as articles" for updates.

### Submission Criteria And Policy

City & State accepts or rejects an assignment within 2 weeks. They use a written contract and acquire all rights.

They accept simultaneous submissions if article is rewritten. They request photos on occasion, with payment negotiable.

### Publication Buys Freelance Submissions On...

| Category | Min. Words | Max. Words | Min. Pay. | Max. Pay. | Per | Cont. |
|---|---|---|---|---|---|---|
| News | 800 | 1000 |  | $10.50 | Inch |  |
| Feature Stories | 800 | 1000 |  | $10.50 | Inch |  |

### Advice for Writers:
"Style sheet is supplied to writers assigned. We generally use AP and our style for specifics."

### Editorial Comments:
"Stories have to be about state and local government."

# Magazines

## Confetti

*Bimonthly Magazine for Comm.*

Randall Publishing Co., Inc.
1425 Lunt Avenue
Elk Grove Village, IL 60007
708-437-6604

### Payment Information

| | |
|---|---|
| Advance paid .................. None | Kill Fee .................. 50% |

Expenses paid

| | | | |
|---|---|---|---|
| ........Y.......... | Travel | ........N........ | Fax |
| ........Y.......... | Overnight Del. | ........Y...... | Phone |

Payment is 100% on acceptance. No payment for rewrites, syndication, reprints or resales, although they provide 100 tear sheets and six copies of the magazine in the case of syndication, reprint or resale.

### Submission Criteria And Policy

Confetti considers unsolicited manuscripts, and accepts or rejects an assignment in 6 to 8 weeks. They use a verbal contract, and rights are "to be discussed with author."

Confetti does not accept simultaneous submissions. "We want fresh, original ideas and do not want to see the same or similar piece appear in a competitive magazine." They accept proposals for articles over the telephone.

### Publication Buys Freelance Submissions On...

| Category | Min. Words | Max. Words | Min. Pay. | Max. Pay. | Per | Cont. |
|---|---|---|---|---|---|---|
| Departmental | | 1200 | | $100.00 | Story | P. Short |
| Feature Stories | 1200 | 2500 | | $100.00 | Story | P. Short |

### Advice for Writers:

"Ask for a copy. Study types of articles. Send samples of your previous work."

# Magazines

**Editorial Comments:**
They pay other expenses "prearranged with editor." They may "require written information of new author" for proposals made over the telephone. They didn't indicate if they pay for updates.

# Magazines

## Consumers Digest
Monthly Consumer Magazine

5705 N. Lincoln Ave.
Chicago, IL 60659
312-275-3590

### Payment Information

Advance paid .................. None      Kill Fee .................. 50%

Expenses paid

..... N ......... Travel           ..... N ......... Fax

..... N ......... Overnight Del.   ..... N ......... Phone

Payment is 30 days after acceptance. No payment for rewrites or updates, as "it happens infrequently." Payment for syndication, reprints or resales depends on the contract.

### Submission Criteria And Policy

Consumers Digest accepts or rejects an assignment in 5 to 30 days. They use a written contract and usually take all rights, but "negotiate with authors."

They accept simultaneous submissions, if notified. Regarding changes to writers' work, the magazine writes "it varies according to article subject—we send galleys on technical subjects, otherwise casual consultation."

### Publication Buys Freelance Submissions On...

| Category | Min. Words | Max. Words | Min. Pay. | Max. Pay. | Per | Cont. |
|---|---|---|---|---|---|---|
| Feature Stories | 1500 | 4000 | $100.00 | $2500.00 | Story | |

# Magazines

### Advice for Writers:
"We have a flexible policy regarding rights—no author who wanted First North American Serial rights has been denied it; most articles reprinted from Consumers Digest involve compensation for the writer, as well."

### Editorial Comments:
They pay other expenses "prearranged with editor." They may "require written information of new author" for proposals made over the telephone.

# Newspapers

## Crain's Chicago Business
Weekly Newspaper

Crain Communications
740 N. Rush Street
Chicago, IL 60611
312-649-5411

### Payment Information

Advance paid .................. None     Kill Fee ...See Comments

Expenses paid

........N.......... Travel        .......N........... Fax

........N.......... Overnight Del.   .......Y....... Phone

Payment is 100% on acceptance. No payment for rewrites, updates, syndication, reprints or resales.

### Submission Criteria And Policy

Crain's Chicago Business does not consider unsolicited manuscripts, and accepts or rejects an assignment within 2 weeks. They use a written contract, and acquire all rights.

Crain's does not accept simultaneous submissions or proposals for articles over the telephone.

### Publication Buys Freelance Submissions On...

| Category | Min. Words | Max. Words | Min. Pay. | Max. Pay. | Per | Cont. |
|---|---|---|---|---|---|---|
| News | | | $11.00 | $12.50 | Inch | B. Reed |
| Feature Stories | | | $11.00 | $12.50 | Inch | G. Coleman |
| Opinion Pieces | | | $11.00 | $12.50 | Inch | M. Miller |

### Editorial Comments:
They don't indicate the length for the categories they buy. Sample copies of the publication are available for $2.50 each. They didn't say if they pay a kill fee.

# Newspapers

## Crain's Small Business
*Business Quarterly*

Crain Communications
740 N. Rush
Chicago, IL 60611
312-649-5411

**Payment Information**

Advance paid .................. None     Kill Fee .................None

Expenses paid

.........N......... Travel              .......N........ Fax

.........N......... Overnight Del.      .......Y...... Phone

Payment is 100% on acceptance. No payment for rewrites, syndication, reprints or resales, but they do pay for updates.

**Submission Criteria And Policy**

Crain's Small Business does not consider unsolicited manuscripts, and accepts or rejects an assignment within 2 weeks. They use a written contract, and acquire all rights.

Crain's Small Business does not accept simultaneous submissions or proposals for articles over the telephone.

**Editorial Comments:**
Sample copies of the publication are available for $2.50 each. It takes "a few days" to respond to queries.

# Magazines

## Discovery YMCA
Association Quarterly

YMCA of the U.S.A.
101 N. Wacker Drive
Chicago, IL 60606
312-977-0031

---
**Payment Information**

Advance paid .................. None     Kill Fee .................None

Expenses paid
........Y.......... Travel              ........Y........ Fax
........Y.......... Overnight Del.      ........Y...... Phone

---

Payment is 100% on submission. No payment for rewrites or updates; they do pay 100% for syndication, reprints, and resales.

### Submission Criteria And Policy

Discovery YMCA considers unsolicited manuscripts. They use a written contract.

They do not accept proposals for articles over the telephone.

### Publication Buys Freelance Submissions On...

| Category | Min. Words | Max. Words | Min. Pay. | Max. Pay. | Per | Cont. |
|---|---|---|---|---|---|---|
| Feature Stories | 1500 | 2500 | | $550.00 | Story | T. Ripley |

### Advice for Writers:
"We almost never accept blind submissions. Send us a pitch letter, resume and clips before submitting a completed story."

### Editorial Comments:
"Discovery YMCA is a feature magazine aimed at Y volunteers and staff members. Our features focus on innovative community-service programs." Their survey response indicated they buy First North American Serial rights, but the contract stipulates "work for hire." They did not reply as to whether they accept simultaneous submissions.

# Magazines

## Electric Light and Power
Monthly Trade Magazine

PennWell Publishing
1250 S. Grove Ave., #302
Barrington, IL 60010
708-382-2450

### Payment Information

Advance paid .................. None      Kill Fee ...See Comments

Expenses paid

.................. Travel           .................. Fax

.................. Overnight Del.   .................. Phone

### Submission Criteria And Policy

Electric Light & Power considers unsolicited manuscripts, uses a verbal contract, and claims all rights.

Electric Light & Power accepts simultaneous submissions.

### Editorial Comments:

The survey did not indicate if the magazine accepts proposals over the telephone. They offered little in the way of submission criteria. They have no policy on expenses, and didn't indicate how long it takes to accept or reject an assignment.

# Magazines

## The Elks Magazine
*Monthly Association Magazine*

425 W. Diversey Pkwy.
Chicago, IL 60614
312-528-4500

### Payment Information

Advance paid .................. None       Kill Fee ................None

Expenses paid

.....N.......... Travel            .....N......... Fax

.....N.......... Overnight Del.    .....N......... Phone

Payment is 100% on acceptance. They do not pay for rewrites and updates. Regarding pay for syndication, reprints or resales, "all rights revert to author upon publication. Requests to reprint are forwarded to author."

### Submission Criteria And Policy

Buys First North American Serial rights. Stories are accepted or rejected usually within 6 weeks. No contracts are used.

Elk Magazine accepts simultaneous submissions.

### Publication Buys Freelance Submissions On...

| Category | Min. Words | Max. Words | Min. Pay. | Max. Pay. | Per | Cont. |
|---|---|---|---|---|---|---|
| Feature Stories | 1200 | 3000 | $.10 | $.15 | Word | |

### Editorial Comments:

"If a piece lends itself to photo illustration, we will ask if photos are available. Depending on the photo, we will pay up to $50." Also, the magazine does not pay kill fees because "everything is done on spec."

# Magazines

**Facets**

*Bimonthly Association Magazine*

**American Medical Association Auxiliary**
535 N. Dearborn Street
Chicago, IL 60610
312-464-0183

### Payment Information

Advance paid .................. None    Kill Fee .................None

Expenses paid

........N.......... Travel    ........Y........ Fax

........Y.......... Overnight Del.    ........Y..... Phone

Payment is 100% on acceptance. No payment for rewrites, updates, syndication, reprints or resales.

### Submission Criteria And Policy

Facets does not consider unsolicited manuscripts, and accepts or rejects an assignment in 1 to 2 weeks. They use a verbal contract, and acquire First North American Serial rights.

Facets does not accept simultaneous submissions or proposals for articles over the telephone.

### Publication Buys Freelance Submissions On...

| Category | Min. Words | Max. Words | Min. Pay. | Max. Pay. | Per | Cont. |
|---|---|---|---|---|---|---|
| Feature Stories | 1000 | 2000 | $600.00 | $800.00 | Story | K. Jordan |

### Advice for Writers:

"We rarely use unsolicited manuscripts. However, we are always interested in good freelancers with queries for articles on health and physicians' family concerns."

# Magazines

**Fancy Food**

*Monthly Trade Magazine*

Talcott Communication Corp.
206 W. Huron
Chicago, IL 60610
312-849-2220

| Payment Information | | | |
|---|---|---|---|
| Advance paid ............... None | | Kill Fee ............... None | |
| Expenses paid | | | |
| ........N.......... | Travel | ........N........ | Fax |
| ........N.......... | Overnight Del. | ........Y...... | Phone |

Payment is 100% on publication. No payment for rewrites or updates; they don't indicate pay for syndication, reprints or resales.

## Submission Criteria And Policy

Fancy Food does not consider unsolicited manuscripts, and accepts or rejects an assignment within a week. They do not use a contract, and acquire one-time rights.

Fancy Food accepts simultaneous submissions. They do not accept proposals for articles over the telephone.

## Publication Buys Freelance Submissions On...

| Category | Min. Words | Max. Words | Min. Pay. | Max. Pay. | Per | Cont. |
|---|---|---|---|---|---|---|
| Feature Stories | 2000 | 2750 | $175.00 | $225.00 | Story | A. Vaughn |

## Editorial Comments:

Sample copies are available for $3 each. It takes one week to review manuscripts. The magazine's field is specialty/gourmet foods.

# Newspapers

**Floral & Nursery Times**
*Semi-monthly Tabloid*

436 Frontage Rd.
Northfield, IL 60093
708-441-0300

### Payment Information

Advance paid .................. None      Kill Fee .................None

Expenses paid

........N.......... Travel         .......N........ Fax

........N.......... Overnight Del.    .......N....... Phone

Payment is 100% on publication. No payment for rewrites, updates, syndication, reprints or resales.

### Submission Criteria And Policy

Floral & Nursery Times considers unsolicited manuscripts, and accepts or rejects an assignment within two weeks. They claim various rights but do not use written contracts.

Floral & Nursery Times does not accept simultaneous submissions. They accept proposals for articles over the telephone.

### Publication Buys Freelance Submissions On...

| Category | Min. Words | Max. Words | Min. Pay. | Max. Pay. | Per | Cont. |
|---|---|---|---|---|---|---|
| Feature Stories | | | $100.00 | $150.00 | Story | B. Gilbert |

### Editorial Comments:
They indicate the length of the features is "optional."

# Newspapers

**Fra Noi**

*Monthly Newspaper*

263 N. York Road
Elmhurst, IL 60126
708-782-4440

### Payment Information

Advance paid .................. None          Kill Fee .................None

Expenses paid

........N.......... Travel              ........N........ Fax

........N.......... Overnight Del.      ........N...... Phone

Fra Noi pays for rewrites and for updates. The amount of payment for syndication, reprints and resales "varies, but is less than usual rate."

### Submission Criteria And Policy

Fra Noi considers unsolicited manuscripts. They do not use a contract.

Fra Noi accepts simultaneous submissions. They accept proposals for articles over the telephone.

### Publication Buys Freelance Submissions On...

| Category | Min. Words | Max. Words | Min. Pay. | Max. Pay. | Per | Cont. |
|---|---|---|---|---|---|---|
| News | 750 | 1500 | $50.00 | $100.00 | Story | P. Basile |
| Feature Stories | 750 | 2500 | $50.00 | $150.00 | Story | P. Basile |
| Reviews | 750 | | $50.00 | | Story | P. Basile |
| Opinion Pieces | 750 | 1500 | | | | |

### Advice for Writers:

"Get clearance for an idea before going ahead with it."

# Newspapers

**Editorial Comments:**
They pay expenses "rarely, and only at the discretion of the editor." They do not indicate how long it takes to respond to a query or review manuscripts. The most frequently covered topics are "anything Italian-American." They do not acquire any rights and pay "100% two months after publication." Sample copies are available at no cost.

# Magazines

## Gay Chicago
*Entertainment & Lifestyle Weekly Mag.*

3121 N. Broadway
Chicago, IL 60057
312-327-7271

### Payment Information

Advance paid ................. None      Kill Fee ................. None

Expenses paid

................. Travel      ................. Fax

................. Overnight Del.      ............. Phone

On contracted pieces, expenses are negotiable. Payment is 100% on publication. No payment for rewrites or updates. Payment for syndication, reprints and resales is negotiable.

### Submission Criteria And Policy

They accept or reject an assignment in one month with SASE. They use a verbal contract and acquire various rights.

Regarding changes to writers' work, "we do light editing and consult for major changes." Gay Chicago does not accept simultaneous submissions. "We want exclusivity in Chicago."

They sometimes ask writers to provide photographs; payment is negotiable.

### Publication Buys Freelance Submissions On...

| Category | Min. Words | Max. Words | Min. Pay. | Max. Pay. | Per | Cont. |
|---|---|---|---|---|---|---|
| Theatre Reviews | 500 | 1000 | $150.00 | $350.00 | Story | |
| Book Reviews | | | $25.00 | $50.00 | Story | |
| Music reviews | | | $25.00 | $50.00 | Story | |
| Entertainment and Lifestyle | | | $25.00 | $50.00 | Story | |
| Feature Stories | 500 | 1000 | $150.00 | $350.00 | Story | |

### Editorial Comments:

"We are an entertainment and lifestyle weekly for the lesbian and gay community."

# Newspapers

## Grocery Marketing

*Semi-monthly Trade Paper*

Delta Communications
455 N. Cityfront Plaza Drive
Chicago, IL 60611
312-222-2000

---

**Payment Information**

Advance paid .................. None        Kill Fee .................None

Expenses paid

.........Y......... Travel                     .........N....... Fax

.........N......... Overnight Del.         .........Y..... Phone

---

Payment is 100% on acceptance. No payment for rewrites, updates, syndication, reprints or resales.

### Submission Criteria And Policy

They accept or reject an assignment in 2 to 4 weeks. They use a verbal contract and acquire various rights.

Grocery Marketing does not accept simultaneous submissions. "We want exclusivity in our trade channel." They accept proposals for articles over the telephone.

They ask writers to provide photographs; payment is negotiable.

### Publication Buys Freelance Submissions On...

| Category | Min. Words | Max. Words | Min. Pay. | Max. Pay. | Per | Cont. |
|---|---|---|---|---|---|---|
| News | | | $100.00 | $300.00 | Story | J. Friedrick |
| Feature Stories | | | $100.00 | $300.00 | Story | J. Friedrick |

### Editorial Comments:

The survey stated they did accept freelance work, but "rarely."

# Magazines

## Illinois Legal Times
Monthly Tabloid

Giant Steps Publishing Corp.
222 Merchandise Mart
Plaza, #1513
Chicago, IL 60650
312-644-4378

### Payment Information

Advance paid ................ None     Kill Fee ................N/A

Expenses paid

........N.......... Travel      ........N........ Fax

........N.......... Overnight Del.     ........N........ Phone

Payment is 100% on publication. Regarding payment for rewrites and updates, they answered "yes and no." No payment for syndication, reprints or resales.

### Submission Criteria And Policy

Illinois Legal Times does not consider unsolicited manuscripts. They accept or reject an assignment in 4 to 8 weeks. They use a written contract and acquire all rights.

Illinois Legal Times does not accept simultaneous submissions. They accept proposals for articles over the telephone.

### Publication Buys Freelance Submissions On...

| Category | Min. Pages | Max. Pages | Min. Pay. | Max. Pay. | Per | Cont. |
|---|---|---|---|---|---|---|
| Feature Stories | 5 | 10 | $50.00 | $80.00 | Story | Kelly Fox |

### Editorial Comments:

In answer to the question about a kill fee, the survey respondent answered, "If we commission a story, we always run it."

# Magazines

## Illinois Medicine
*Professional Fortnightly*

Illinois State Medical Society
20 N. Michigan, #700
Chicago, IL 60602
312-782-1654

| Payment Information |
|---|
| Advance paid .................. None     Kill Fee .................. 33% |
| Expenses paid |
| ........N.......... Travel          ......Y......... Fax |
| ........Y.......... Overnight Del.   ......Y........ Phone |

Payment is 100% on acceptance. They pay for updates, and sometimes pay for rewrites, depending "on circumstances." No payment for syndication, reprints or resales.

### Submission Criteria And Policy

Illinois Medicine does not consider unsolicited manuscripts, and accepts or rejects an assignment within a week. They use a written contract and acquire one-time rights.

Illinois Medicine accepts simultaneous submission "as long as it is only a proposal." They accept proposals for articles over the telephone.

### Publication Buys Freelance Submissions On...

| Category | Min. Words | Max. Words | Min. Pay. | Max. Pay. | Per | Cont. |
|---|---|---|---|---|---|---|
| News | 600 | 1000 | $240.00 | $400.00 | C | L. Koslowsky |
| Feature Stories | 800 | 1000 | $320.00 | $400.00 | C | L. Koslowsky |

### Advice for Writers:
"Know about the publication or learn about it—its slant, purpose, readers and important issues."

# Magazines

## Inland Architect
*Bimonthly Professional Magazine*

Inland Architect Press
P. O. Box 10394
Chicago, IL 60610
312-465-5151

---

**Payment Information**

Advance paid ................. None      Kill Fee ................. 50%

Expenses paid

.........N......... Travel      .........N..... Fax

.........Y......... Overnight Del.      .........Y...... Phone

---

Payment is 100% on publication. No payment for rewrites, updates, syndication, reprints or resales.

### Submission Criteria And Policy

Inland Architect considers unsolicited manuscripts, and accepts or rejects an assignment in 6 to 8 weeks. They use a verbal contract.

Inland Architect does not accept simultaneous submissions. "We don't want an article withdrawn if the author chooses to go with a competing publication." They accept proposals for articles over the telephone.

### Publication Buys Freelance Submissions On...

| Category | Min. Words | Max. Words | Min. Pay. | Max. Pay. | Per | Cont. |
|---|---|---|---|---|---|---|
| Feature Stories | 2500 | 5000 | $150.00 | | Story | |
| Book Reviews | 500 | 1000 | $50.00 | | Story | |
| Departmental | 500 | 1500 | $125.00 | | Story | |

### Advice for Writers:
Propose a specific topic—to cover a lecture/exhibit, write about a new or proposed project. Articles must be written for an audience consisting primarily of well-educated architects.

### Editorial Comments:
They pay for travel "occasionally." They usually use a verbal contract, "sometimes with a letter."

# Magazines

## In These Times
*Biweekly Newsmagazine*

2040 N. Milwaukee Avenue
Chicago, IL 60647
312-772-0100

### Payment Information

Advance paid ................... None          Kill Fee ........... Variable

Expenses paid

................... Travel                    ................ Fax

................... Overnight Del.             ............ Phone

In These Times had a contract with the National Writers Union that the magazine violated frequently.

The magazine supposedly paid 100% on acceptance, but writers complained that payments were held up for months or even years. Extensive negotiations between the NWU and ITT have resulted in the promise of payment of all back debts.

### Submission Criteria And Policy

ITT considers unsolicited manuscripts. The publication buys First North American Serial rights only, unless the writer authorizes ITT to sell reprint rights. Pay is negotiable.

### Publication Buys Freelance Submissions On...

| Category | Min. Words | Max. Words | Min. Pay. | Max. Pay. | Per | Cont. |
|---|---|---|---|---|---|---|
| News | 500 | 1000 | $150.00 | $350.00 | Story | |
| Feature Stories | 500 | 1000 | $150.00 | $350.00 | Story | |
| TV Technology | 500 | 1000 | $150.00 | $350.00 | Story | |

# Magazines

**Editorial Comments:**
In the past, this supposedly pro-labor publication has generated a large number of complaints for non-payment, according to NWU grievance officials.

# Newspapers

**Joliet Herald-News**
Daily Newspaper

300 Caterpillar Drive
Joliet, IL 60436
815-729-6047

---

**Payment Information**

Advance paid .................. None     Kill Fee ................None

Expenses paid

........N.......... Travel         .......N......... Fax

.........N.......... Overnight Del.   .......N....... Phone

---

No payment for rewrites, updates, syndication, reprints or resales.

**Submission Criteria And Policy**

Joliet Herald-News considers unsolicited manuscripts, and accepts or rejects an assignment in 1 to 4 weeks. They acquire one-time rights and use a written contract.

Joliet Herald-News accepts both simultaneous submissions and proposals for articles over the telephone.

They ask writers to provide photographs. Payment is $25-$35. They may omit the author's byline.

**Publication Buys Freelance Submissions On...**

| Category | Min. Inches | Max. Inches | Min. Pay. | Max. Pay. | Per | Cont. |
|---|---|---|---|---|---|---|
| News | 1 | 18 | $5.00 | $40.00 | Inch | J. Larsen |
| Feature Stories | 6 | 50 | $5.00 | $75.00 | Inch | J. Larsen |

**Advice for Writers:**
"Be accurate. Be brief. Understand why we rewrite if we have to."

**Editorial Comments:**
They "do not syndicate or reprint freelance work." They don't indicate when they pay. They may buy by the inch (1-18 inches for a news story), but pay by the story ($5-$40 for a news story).

# Magazines

## Journal of Property Management
*Bimonthly Trade Magazine*

Institute of Real Estate Management
430 N. Michigan Ave., Box 109025
Chicago, IL 60611-9025
312-329-6000

### Payment Information

Advance paid ................. None      Kill Fee ................. 30%

Expenses paid

..........N......... Travel        .......Y......... Fax

..........Y......... Overnight Del.      .......Y....... Phone

Payment is 100% on acceptance. No payment for rewrites, syndication, reprints or resales, but they do pay for updates.

### Submission Criteria And Policy

Journal of Property Management considers unsolicited manuscripts, and accepts or rejects an assignment within 3 weeks. They use a written contract and acquire all rights.

Journal of Property Management does not accept simultaneous submissions. "Writers do not tell you, and you end up accepting an article that has run elsewhere." They do not accept proposals for articles over the telephone.

They do not ask writers to provide photographs.

### Publication Buys Freelance Submissions On...

| Category | Min. Words | Max. Words | Min. Pay. | Max. Pay. | Per | Cont. |
|---|---|---|---|---|---|---|
| Departmental | 500 | 1000 | $300.00 | $500.00 | Story | M. Schindler |
| Feature Stories | 1500 | 3000 | $600.00 | $1000.00 | Story | M. Evans |

### Advice for Writers:
"Learn the needs of our very specialized market."

# Magazines

## Law Practice Management
*Bimonthly Magazine*

American Bar Association
750 N. Lake Shore Drive
Chicago, IL 60611
312-988-5000

### Payment Information

Advance paid .................. None          Kill Fee ................None

Expenses paid

........N.......... Travel                   .......N....... Fax

........N.......... Overnight Del.           ........N...... Phone

Payment is 100% on publication. They do not pay for rewrites, updates, syndication, reprints or resales.

### Submission Criteria And Policy

Law Practice Management considers unsolicited manuscripts. They do not use a contract, yet claim various rights. Law Practice Management accepts simultaneous submissions. "If accepted elsewhere, we will not publish." They accept proposals for articles over the telephone

### Publication Buys Freelance Submissions On...

| Category | Min. Words | Max. Words | Min. Pay. | Max. Pay. | Per | Cont. |
|---|---|---|---|---|---|---|
| Feature Stories | 500 | 7500 | $200.00 | $350.00 | Story | H. Hatoff |

### Advice for Writers:
"We are an official publication of the American Bar Association. We do not make it a practice of seeking articles from paid professional writers due to budget. Most articles come from volunteers."

### Editorial Comments:
Sample copies are available. The time it takes to review manuscripts "depends—editorial board meets 4 times a year." It takes 1 to 2 weeks to respond to a query. Fields covered are "managing law firms" and "technology for law firms." The most frequently covered topics are "marketing, billing, personnel issues."

# Magazines

**The Lion Magazine**
*Association Monthly*

Lions Clubs International
300 W. 22nd Street
Oak Brook, IL 60521
708-571-5466

---

**Payment Information**

Advance paid .................. None      Kill Fee .................. 50%

Expenses paid

    ........N.......... Travel           ........Y..... Fax

    ........N.......... Overnight Del.   ........Y...... Phone

---

Payment is 100% on acceptance. No payment for rewrites (they are generally staff-generated), syndication, reprints or resales. They pay 25-50% for updates.

### Submission Criteria And Policy

The Lion considers unsolicited manuscripts, and accepts or rejects an assignment in 2 to 3 weeks. They use a written contract and acquire various rights.

The Lion accepts simultaneous submissions and they accept proposals for articles over the telephone.

### Publication Buys Freelance Submissions On...

| Category | Min. Words | Max. Words | Min. Pay. | Max. Pay. | Per | Cont. |
|---|---|---|---|---|---|---|
| Feature Stories | 1000 | 2500 | $300.00 | $750.00 | Story | B. Kleindelder |
| News | 500 | 2500 | $150.00 | $750.00 | Story | B. Kleinfelder |

### Advice for Writers:

Understand the type of material The Lion uses. Free sample copies and writers' guidelines are sent on request.

### Editorial Comments:

The news category includes news about Lions Club service and fund-raising projects. Their contract is a letter of acceptance for the manuscript and claims "all magazine publication rights." Payment for photographs is "included as part of total fee."

# Newspapers

**Logan Square Extra**
Weekly Newspaper

Extra Community Newspapers
3918 W. North Ave.
Chicago, IL 60647
312-252-3534

---
**Payment Information**

Advance paid .................. None     Kill Fee .................None

Expenses paid

........N.......... Travel          ........Y........ Fax

........N.......... Overnight Del.   ........Y...... Phone

---

Payment is 100% on publication. No payment for syndication or reprints, but they do pay an unspecified amount for rewrites and updates, and 50% for resales.

### Submission Criteria And Policy

Logan Square Extra considers unsolicited manuscripts, and accepts or rejects an assignment within 2 weeks. They do not use a contract and claim First North American Serial rights.

Logan Square Extra accepts simultaneous submissions. They accept proposals for articles over the telephone.

They ask writers to provide photographs; payment is $25. Advances for expenses range from $10 to $25.

### Publication Buys Freelance Submissions On...

| Category | Min. Inches | Max. Inches | Min. Pay. | Max. Pay. | Per | Cont. |
|---|---|---|---|---|---|---|
| News | 1 | 1.5 | $1.50 | $5.00 | Inch | M. Alba |
| Departmental | 1 | 1.5 | $1.50 | $5.00 | Inch | M. Alba |

# Newspapers

**Advice for Writers:**
"The Logan Square Extra serves Chicago's Hispanic community. All articles must have this type of slant to them. Submissions in English."

**Editorial Comments:**
Editor indicates "there are seven publications under the Extra banner. All editions are bilingual (Spanish/English)."

# Magazines

**The Lutheran**

*Monthly Religious Magazine*

8765 W. Higgins Road
Chicago, IL 60631
312-380-2540

### Payment Information

Advance paid .................. None          Kill Fee .................. 50%

Expenses paid

........Y.......... Travel           .......Y........ Fax

........Y.......... Overnight Del.   .......Y....... Phone

Payment is 100% on acceptance. They do not pay for rewrites but pay for updates. Syndication, reprints and resale payments are negotiable.

### Submission Criteria And Policy

The Lutheran considers unsolicited manuscripts. They respond to queries within 3 weeks and to articles within 3 months. They don't use a contract and acquire First North American Serial rights.

The Lutheran does not accept simultaneous submissions. "No explicit policy, but we have never done it." They do not accept proposals for articles over the telephone.

They ask writers to provide photographs. Payment is "negotiated."

### Publication Buys Freelance Submissions On...

| Category | Min. Words | Max. Words | Min. Pay. | Max. Pay. | Per | Cont. |
|---|---|---|---|---|---|---|
| Feature Stories | 500 | 2000 | $50.00 | $600.00 | Story | D. Miller |

### Advice for Writers:
"No articles unrelated to the world of religion."

### Editorial Comments:
Free sample copies are available.

96

# Magazines

## Maintenance Technology
*Monthly Tabloid*

Applied Technology Publications
1300 S. Grove Ave., Suite 205
Barrington, IL 60010
708-382-8100

### Payment Information

Advance paid .................. None     Kill Fee .................None

Expenses paid

........Y.......... Travel              .......Y....... Fax

.........Y......... Overnight Del.      .......Y....... Phone

Payment is 100% on acceptance. No payment for rewrites, updates, syndication, reprints or resales.

### Submission Criteria And Policy

Maintenance Technology uses an exchange of letters as their contract and acquires all rights.

They do not accept simultaneous submissions. "We want exclusive material."

Depending on the piece they will ask writers for photos or illustrations, with no additional payment.

### Publication Buys Freelance Submissions On...

| Category | Min. Words | Max. Words | Min. Payment | Max. Payment | Per |
|---|---|---|---|---|---|
| Feature Stories | Negotiable—contact Robert Baldwin | | | | |

### Advice for Writers:

"As with all technical business magazines, the writer must know as much as, if not more than the reader, or you have no chance of getting anything accomplished."

# Magazines

**Editorial Comments:**
The magazine looks for technical and management topics, on assignment only. They will sometimes publish third-party stories (stories that the magazine receives from companies who hire an outside party to write the piece). In this case, they ask for First North American Serial rights only; otherwise they ask for all rights. They do not pay for rewrites, preferring to accept the story if it's good and rewrite it themselves. Allow an acceptance period of one week for expected articles and several weeks for over-the-transom articles.

# Newspapers

## Marketing News
*Biweekly Trade Newspaper*

250 S. Wacker Drive, #200
Chicago, IL 60606-5819
312-993-9517

---

**Payment Information**

Advance paid .................. None     Kill Fee ..See Comments

Expenses paid
.........N........ Travel          .......N...... Fax
.........N......... Overnight Del.  .......Y....... Phone

---

Payment is 100% on acceptance. No payment for rewrites, updates, syndication, reprints or resales.

### Submission Criteria And Policy

Marketing News does not consider unsolicited manuscripts. See Comments for time needed to accept or reject an assignment. They use a written contract and acquire various rights.

Marketing News does not accept simultaneous submissions. "We don't like bidding wars." They accept proposals for articles over the telephone.

### Publication Buys Freelance Submissions On...

| Category | Min. Words | Max. Words | Min. Pay. | Max. Pay. | Per | Cont. |
|---|---|---|---|---|---|---|
| News | 1500 | 1500 | See Comments | | Story | G. Cebrzynski |
| Feature Stories | 1500 | 1500 | See Comments | | Story | G. Cebrzynski |

### Advice for Writers:
"Stories should have a strong marketing angle and [be] geared toward marketers, not consumers."

# Newspapers

**Editorial Comments:**
"We're generally first with important stories, so don't propose something too big; we've probably done it." The most frequently covered topics: "everything dealing with marketing and marketing research." All rates are "negotiable." They pay a percentage of total payment as a kill fee "when the piece is so bad it can't be rewritten. Such cases are rare." The time needed to respond to a query and accept/reject a manuscript is "within a day or two." One free sample copy is available to professional writers.

# Newspapers

**N'digo**
Monthly Tabloid

325 W. Huron St.
Chicago, IL 60610
312-587-2600

## Payment Information

Advance paid ................... $75       Kill Fee ................None

Expenses paid

................... Travel                ................... Fax

................... Overnight Del.        ............ Phone

Payment is 100% on publication. No payment for rewrites or updates, but they do pay 10% for syndication, 15% for reprints and 50% for resales.

### Submission Criteria And Policy

N'Digo acquires various rights and uses a verbal contract.

N'Digo does not accept simultaneous submissions. "We want exclusive material." They accept proposals for articles over the telephone.

They ask writers to provide photographs. Payment is $20.

### Publication Buys Freelance Submissions On...

| Category | Minimum Words | Maximum Words | Minimum Payment | Maximum Payment | Per |
|---|---|---|---|---|---|
| News | 500 | | See Comments | | |
| Feature Stories | 1000 | | See Comments | | |
| Book Reviews | 300 | | See Comments | | |
| Music Reviews | 300 | | See Comments | | |
| Theatre Reviews | 300 | | See Comments | | |
| Film Reviews | 300 | | See Comments | | |

### Advice for Writers:
"To write well. We are interested in stories on and about African-Americans."

### Editorial Comments:
They do not indicate the rates they pay, whether or not they pay any expenses, or how long it takes to accept or reject an assignment.

# Magazines

## Neighborhood Works
*Community Advocacy Bimonthly*

2125 W. North Ave.
Chicago, IL 60647
312-278-4800

### Payment Information

Advance paid .................. None          Kill Fee .................. Neg.

Expenses paid

........N.......... Travel            .......N.......... Fax

........N.......... Overnight Del.    .......Y....... Phone

Payment is 100% on publication. No payment for rewrites, but they do pay for updates. Survey respondent did not indicate if they pay for syndication, reprints or resales.

### Submission Criteria And Policy

Neighborhood Works considers unsolicited manuscripts, and accepts or rejects an assignment in 1 to 4 weeks. They use a written contract and acquire various rights.

Neighborhood Works accepts simultaneous submissions and accepts proposals for articles over the telephone.

See Comments for information about photographs.

### Publication Buys Freelance Submissions On...

| Category | Min. Words | Max. Words | Min. Pay. | Max. Pay. | Per | Cont. |
|---|---|---|---|---|---|---|
| News | 750 | 2500 | $50.00 | $400.00 | Story | M. O'Connell |
| Opinion Pieces | 750 | 1000 | See Comments | | Story | M. O'Connell |
| Book Reviews | 750 | 1000 | See Comments | | Story | M. O'Connell |

### Advice for Writers:

"Read The Neighborhood Works. Emphasize the community organizing angle—don't talk to the mayor about the city's new housing program, talk to the community groups that designed it and fought for it."

# Magazines

**Editorial Comments:**
They ask for photos and pay for "cost of film, production." Payment for book reviews and opinion pieces is "negotiable."

# Magazines

## New Art Examiner
*Art Monthly*

1255 S. Wabash, 4th Floor
Chicago, IL 60605
312-786-0200

### Payment Information

Advance paid .................. None        Kill Fee .................None

Expenses paid

........Y.......... Travel              .......Y....... Fax

........Y.......... Overnight Del.      .......Y....... Phone

Payment is 100% on publication. No payment for rewrites or updates. The survey respondent didn't indicate if they pay for syndication, reprints or resales.

### Submission Criteria And Policy

New Art Examiner considers unsolicited manuscripts, and accepts or rejects an assignment in 1 to 8 weeks. They use a verbal contract and acquire various rights.

New Art Examiner accepts simultaneous submissions. They do not accept proposals for articles over the telephone.

### Publication Buys Freelance Submissions On...

| Category | Min. Words | Max. Words | Min. Pay. | Max. Pay. | Per | Cont. |
|---|---|---|---|---|---|---|
| Reviews | | | | $35.00 | Story | |
| Cover Stories | | | | $300.00 | Story | A. Gamble |
| Columns | | | | $75.00 | Story | |
| Other | | | | $.10 | Word | |

### Advice for Writers:

"As a general rule, the New Art Examiner does not publish unsolicited manuscripts; unsolicited reviews are not accepted. Clips and manuscripts will be reviewed for future assignments. Return only with SASE."

# Newspapers

## New City
*Weekly Newspaper*

770 N. Halsted
Chicago, IL 60610
312-243-8786

### Payment Information

Advance paid ................. None     Kill Fee .................. 25%

Expenses paid

................. Travel     ................. Fax

................. Overnight Del.     ............. Phone

Payment is 100% on publication. No payment for rewrites, but they do pay for updates if it is a separate story. Syndication, reprints and resales are negotiable.

### Submission Criteria And Policy

New City considers unsolicited manuscripts and accepts or rejects an assignment within 4 weeks. They use a verbal contract and acquire various rights.

New City does not accept simultaneous submissions. "We react quickly and don't want to waste time with a piece that may not be available." They do not accept proposals for articles over the telephone.

### Publication Buys Freelance Submissions On...

| Category | Min. Words | Max. Words | Min. Pay. | Max. Pay. | Per | Cont. |
|---|---|---|---|---|---|---|
| News | 100 | 1500 | $10.00 | $150.00 | Story | B. Hieggelke |
| Feature Stories | 750 | 900 | | $75.00 | Story | B. Hieggelke |
| Music Reviews | | 175 | | $15.00 | Story | B. Hieggelke |
| Book Reviews | | 175 | | $15.00 | Story | B. Hieggelke |
| Theatre Reviews | | 175 | | $15.00 | Story | B. Hieggelke |
| Film Reviews | | 175 | | $15.00 | Story | B. Hieggelke |
| Cover Stories | 2000 | 3000 | $200.00 | | Story | B. Hieggelke |

# Newspapers

**Advice for Writers:**
"Send SASE for freelance guidelines."

**Editorial Comments:**
On certain assignments, they indicate they pay a kill fee up to 100%. They pay "negotiated expenses only."

# Newspapers

**News-Sun**

*Daily Newspaper*

100 W. Madison
Waukegan, IL 60085
708-249-7200

---

### Payment Information

Advance paid .................... None     Kill Fee ................. None

Expenses paid

    ........N.......... Travel      ........N........ Fax

    ........N.......... Overnight Del.      ........N...... Phone

---

Payment is 100% on publication. No payment for rewrites, updates, syndication, reprints or resales.

### Submission Criteria And Policy

News-Sun does not consider unsolicited manuscripts. They don't use a contract, but claim all rights.

News-Sun does not accept simultaneous submissions. They accept proposals for articles over the telephone.

They ask writers to provide photographs. Payment for first photo is $30; second and third photos are $15 and $8, respectively.

### Publication Buys Freelance Submissions On...

| Category | Minimum Words | Maximum Words | Minimum Payment | Maximum Payment | Per |
|---|---|---|---|---|---|
| Feature Stories | | | $30.00 | $50.00 | Story |

# Magazines

## North Shore
*Monthly Consumer Magazine*

PB Communications
874 Green Bay Road
Winnetka, IL 60093
708-441-7892

### Payment Information

Advance paid .................. None      Kill Fee .................. 50%

Expenses paid

.................. Travel           .................. Fax

.................. Overnight Del.    .............. Phone

Payment is usually on acceptance or publication. Payment for rewrites, updates, syndication, reprints and resales "varies."

### Submission Criteria And Policy

North Shore considers unsolicited manuscripts, and accepts or rejects an assignment in 4 to 6 weeks. They acquire various rights. See Comments for contract details.

North Shore accepts simultaneous submissions, but they don't accept proposals for articles over the telephone.

They ask writers to provide photographs.

### Publication Buys Freelance Submissions On...

| Category | Min. Words | Max. Words | Min. Pay. | Max. Pay. | Per | Cont. |
|---|---|---|---|---|---|---|
| News | 500 | 3000 | $100.00 | $600.00 | Story | K. Titus |
| Feature Stories | 500 | 3000 | $100.00 | $600.00 | Story | K. Titus |

### Advice for Writers:
Submit "succinct query letter with 2-3 relevant published clips; familiarity with our region (north and northwest suburbs) is appreciated."

# Magazines

**Editorial Comments:**
They use both verbal and written ("letter of confirmation") contracts. The kill fee is generally 50%. The expenses paid are negotiable. The percentage of payment made upon acceptance and upon publication varies. Payment for photographs also varies.

# Magazines

**Planning Magazine**
Association Monthly

**American Planning Association**
1313 E. 60th Street
Chicago, IL 60637
312-955-9100

### Payment Information

Advance paid .................. None         Kill Fee ...See Comments

Expenses paid

........N.......... Travel              ........N........ Fax

........Y.......... Overnight Del.      ........Y...... Phone

Payment is 100% on publication. They pay for rewrites and updates, but do not indicate if they pay for syndication, reprints or resales.

### Submission Criteria And Policy

Planning Magazine considers unsolicited manuscripts, and accepts or rejects an assignment in 5 weeks. They use a written contract and acquire all rights.

Planning Magazine doesn't mind simultaneous submissions, but wants to be the first to publish any given item. They do not accept proposals for articles over the telephone.

They ask writers to provide photographs. Payment is $65 to $100 per magazine page.

### Publication Buys Freelance Submissions On...

| Category | Min. Words | Max. Words | Min. Pay. | Max. Pay. | Per | Cont. |
|---|---|---|---|---|---|---|
| News | 100 | 300 | $50.00 | $125.00 | Story | M. Gallagher |
| Feature Stories | 1500 | 3000 | $500.00 | $800.00 | Story | S. Lewis |

### Advice for Writers:

"Get three copies of our magazine and give some thought to our audience (city planners nationwide)."

# Magazines

**Editorial Comments:**
One sample copy is available free. The most frequently covered topic is "land development nationwide." They pay a kill fee "if story is totally unsalvageable. Usually, we salvage." Their contracts are individual letters. They respond to queries within 5 weeks.

# Magazines

## Playboy Magazine
*Monthly Consumer Magazine*

680 N. Lake Shore Drive
Chicago, IL 60611
312-751-8000

### Payment Information

Advance paid ............ None      Kill Fee ............ 20%

Expenses paid

........Y.......... Travel          .......N...... Fax

........N.......... Overnight Del.  .......Y...... Phone

Payment is 100% on acceptance. No payment for rewrites or updates, and they don't indicate if they pay for syndication, reprints or resales. Travel and phone expenses are reimbursed.

### Submission Criteria And Policy

Playboy considers unsolicited manuscripts, and accepts or rejects an assignment in 3 to 5 weeks. They use a written contract and acquire all rights.

Playboy does not accept simultaneous submissions or proposals for articles over the telephone.

### Publication Buys Freelance Submissions On...

| Category | Min. Words | Max. Words | Min. Pay. | Max. Pay. | Per | Cont. |
|---|---|---|---|---|---|---|
| Departmental | 100 | 500 | $50.00 | | Story | C. Napolitano |
| Feature Stories | 3000 | 5000 | $3000.00 | | Story | J. Rezek |

### Advice for Writers:
"Know the magazine."

### Editorial Comments:
They use both written and verbal contracts.

# Magazines

## Real Estate Today
*Association Monthly*

National Association of Realtors
430 N. Michigan Ave.
Chicago, IL 60611
312-329-8458

### Payment Information

Advance paid .................. None    Kill Fee .................. 20%

Expenses paid

........N.......... Travel            ........N..... Fax

........N.......... Overnight Del.    ........Y...... Phone

Payment is 100% on acceptance. No payment for rewrites, updates, syndication, reprints or resales. Phone expenses are reimbursed up to $100.

### Submission Criteria And Policy

Real Estate Today does not consider unsolicited manuscripts, and accepts or rejects an assignment within a week. They use a written contract and acquire First North American Serial rights.

Real Estate Today does not accept simultaneous submissions. "Generally, they're not well-tailored to our readers." They do not accept proposals for articles over the telephone.

### Publication Buys Freelance Submissions On...

| Category | Min. Words | Max. Words | Min. Pay. | Max. Pay. | Per | Cont. |
|---|---|---|---|---|---|---|
| Departmental | | | $500.00 | $750.00 | Story | C. Hoffmann |
| Feature Stories | 1500 | 2500 | $1000.00 | $2000.00 | Story | |

### Advice for Writers:

"Read the contract and content guidelines we provide. If you can't do something we've asked for, let us know before you submit the story."

### Editorial Comments:

They indicate that the 20% kill fee is 20% of the minimum payment in the ranges given. Also, payment for the particular story within the range given for that category is "decided on acceptance."

# Magazines

## The Rotarian
*Association Monthly*

Rotary International
One Rotary Center
1500 Sherman Ave.
Evanston, IL 60201
708-866-3000

| Payment Information | |
|---|---|
| Advance paid ................ Neg. | Kill Fee ................Neg. |
| Expenses paid | |
| ........N...... Travel | ........N... Fax |
| ........N....... Overnight Del. | ........N... Phone |

Payment is 100% on acceptance. All payment is negotiable, including expenses, rewrites and updates. Payment for syndication, reprints, or resales varies.

### Submission Criteria And Policy

The Rotarian accepts proposals over the phone but prefers written queries. They accept or reject an assignment within 2 weeks. They use a written contract and acquire various rights. The Rotarian accepts simultaneous submissions.

They do ask writers to provide photographs occasionally, with payment negotiable.

### Advice for Writers:
"Study several issues first for content/style/audience."

### Editorial Comments:
Request editorial guidelines for more specific information.

# Magazines

## Safety & Health
Trade Monthly Assoc. Publication

National Safety Council
1121 Spring Lake Dr.
Itasca, IL 60143-3201
708-775-2279

### Payment Information

Advance paid .................. None      Kill Fee ...See Comments

Expenses paid

.........N......... Travel           ........N..... Fax

.........N......... Overnight Del.   ........Y...... Phone

Payment is 100% on acceptance. They don't pay for updates and don't do syndication or resales, but they do pay $50 for reprints and sometimes pay for rewrites.

### Submission Criteria And Policy

Safety & Health does not consider unsolicited manuscripts. See Comments for information on acceptance and rejection of assignments.

They use a verbal contract and acquire all rights.

Safety & Health does not accept simultaneous submissions. "We assign articles to meet our editorial-calendar needs." They do not accept proposals for articles over the telephone.

They ask writers to provide photographs. Payment is $50 per photo.

### Publication Buys Freelance Submissions On...

| Category | Min. Words | Max. Words | Min. Pay. | Max. Pay. | Per | Cont. |
|---|---|---|---|---|---|---|
| Feature Stories | 1500 | 2000 | | | Story | D. Gaska |

### Advice for Writers:

"Send resume and samples to us. We will call you if interested. Please do not make follow-up calls."

# Magazines

### Editorial Comments:
"We have an editorial calendar to which we closely adhere. Articles for the calendar are assigned 4-5 months in advance of publication." The survey indicated that although they do accept freelance work, they "commission all freelance work. Do not write a story, then send it in to us." It lists the magazine as a trade publication in the field of safety and as an association publication of the National Safety Council. Topics most frequently covered are "OSHA regulations [and] workplace safety issues." The payment for each category "varies." Under a kill fee, the magazine wrote "No comment. Depends on each individual situation. Doesn't happen often that we need to." The amount of time to respond to a query and to accept/reject a manuscript varies. Free sample copies are available.

# Newspapers

**Salt**

*Christian Monthly on Social Justice*

Claretian Publications
205 W. Monroe Street
Chicago, IL 60606
312-236-7782

---

**Payment Information**

Advance paid ............... None        Kill Fee ...See Comments

Expenses paid

........N......... Travel            ........Y...... Fax

........Y......... Overnight Del.    ........Y...... Phone

---

Payment is 100% on acceptance. No payment for updates, syndication, reprints or resales.

### Submission Criteria And Policy

Salt considers unsolicited manuscripts, and accepts or rejects an assignment in 3 to 5 weeks. They use a written contract and acquire First North American Serial rights.

See Comments for simultaneous submissions policy. They do not accept proposals for articles over the telephone.

### Publication Buys Freelance Submissions On...

| Category | Min. Words | Max. Words | Min. Pay. | Max. Pay. | Per | Cont. |
|---|---|---|---|---|---|---|
| Opinion Pieces | 1000 | | $200.00 | | Story | K. Clarke |
| Feature Stories | 2000 | 3500 | $400.00 | $500.00 | Story | M.L. Hendrickson |
| First Per. Profiles | 1200 | | $250.00 | $300.00 | Story | M. Edmunds |

### Advice for Writers:

"Get to know the magazine. We have a specific niche."

# Newspapers

**Editorial Comments:**
Their written contract is a "commissioning letter." They did not indicate the percentage they would pay for the kill fee. They said they would not pay for a rewrite "if a rewrite was for something the writer was supposed to cover but didn't." They frown on simultaneous publication of the same material.

# Magazines

## Stagebill

Monthly Trade Theatre Magazine

4363 W. Montrose
Chicago, IL 60641
312-685-3911

### Payment Information

Advance paid ................. None        Kill Fee ...See Comments

Expenses paid

........N.......... Travel            .......N....... Fax

........Y........ Overnight Del.      .......N....... Phone

Payment is 100% on publication. No payment for rewrites, but they do pay for updates. They do not indicate payment for syndication, reprints or resales.

### Submission Criteria And Policy

Stagebill does not consider unsolicited manuscripts. See Comments for time required to accept or reject assignments. They use a verbal contract and acquire various rights.

Stagebill accepts simultaneous submissions. They accept proposals for articles over the telephone.

### Publication Buys Freelance Submissions On...

| Category | Min. Words | Max. Words | Min. Pay. | Max. Pay. | Per | Cont. |
|---|---|---|---|---|---|---|
| Feature Stories | 500 | 1500 | $75.00 | $325.00 | Story | S. Pine |

### Advice for Writers:

"Do research/homework on publication queried; call or write with concise, well-worded ideas/proposals."

# Magazines

### Editorial Comments:
The most frequently covered topics are "actor profiles, theater features." They pay a flat amount kill fee if the article is pulled after the majority of the assignment is completed. They pay 100% of overnight delivery indicated as an advance. Under length of time to accept/reject a manuscript, they wrote "N/A." They take one week to respond to a query.

# Newspapers

**Standard Rate & Data**

*Semi-annual Trade Directories*

3004 Glenview Road
Wilmette, IL 60091
708-256-6067

---

**Payment Information**

Advance paid .................. None     Kill Fee ................. None

Expenses paid

........N.......... Travel           .......Y......... Fax

.........Y......... Overnight Del.   .....Y...... Phone

---

Payment is 100% on publication. No payment for syndication, reprints or resales, but they do pay for updates.

**Submission Criteria And Policy**

Standard Rate & Data does not consider unsolicited manuscripts and accepts or rejects an assignment in 2 to 6 weeks. They use a verbal contract and claim all rights.

Standard Rate & Data accepts simultaneous submissions. They accept proposals for articles over the telephone.

**Publication Buys Freelance Submissions On...**

| Category | Min. Words | Max. Words | Min. Pay. | Max. Pay. | Per | Cont. |
|---|---|---|---|---|---|---|
| Departmental | | | | | | J. Goss |
| Feature Stories | | | | | | J. Goss |

**Editorial Comments:**

The rates for both "Feature Stories" and "Departmental and other pieces" is given as "variable lengths/negotiable rates."

# Magazines

**Systems Management 3X/400 Magazine**
*Trade Monthly*

25 N. W. Point Blvd.
Suite 800
Elk Grove Village, IL 60007
708-427-9512

### Payment Information

Advance paid .................. None          Kill Fee .................None

Expenses paid

........Y.......... Travel                    .......N....... Fax

........Y.......... Overnight Del.            .......Y....... Phone

Payment is 100% on publication. No payment for rewrites, syndication, reprint or resales, but they do pay for updates.

### Submission Criteria And Policy

Systems Management considers unsolicited manuscripts, and accepts or rejects an assignment in 1 to 4 weeks. They use a verbal contract and claim all rights.

Systems Management accepts simultaneous submissions. They do not accept proposals for articles over the telephone.

### Publication Buys Freelance Submissions On...

| Category | Min. Words | Max. Words | Min. Pay. | Max. Pay. | Per | Cont. |
|---|---|---|---|---|---|---|
| Feature Stories | 1000 | 3000 | $400.00 | $800.00 | Story | |

### Advice for Writers:
"Tailor stories to our audience."

# Magazines

**Telephony**

*Trade Weekly*

Intertec Publishing Corp.
55 E. Jackson Blvd.
Chicago, IL 60604-4188
312-922-2435

---
**Payment Information**

Advance paid .................. None     Kill Fee ..See Comments

Expenses paid

........Y.......... Travel            .......Y....... Fax

........Y.......... Overnight Del.    .......Y....... Phone

---

See Comments for time of payment. No payment for rewrites, syndication, reprints or resales, but they do pay for updates.

**Submission Criteria And Policy**

Telephony considers unsolicited manuscripts, and accepts or rejects an assignment in 1 to 8 weeks. They use a written contract and acquire all rights.

Telephony does not accept simultaneous submissions. "We compete with other magazines for exclusive feature material—simultaneous submission makes that process difficult." They do not accept proposals for articles over the telephone (ironic, given the name of the publication).

They ask writers to provide photographs. See Comments for payment information.

**Publication Buys Freelance Submissions On...**

| Category | Min. Words | Max. Words | Min. Pay. | Max. Pay. | Per | Cont. |
|---|---|---|---|---|---|---|
| News | | | | | Story | S. Titch |
| Feature Stories | 1500 | 2000 | | | Story | C. Wilson |

**Advice for Writers:**
"Read the magazine, understand the readers and focus a written query on that audience."

# Magazines

**Editorial Comments:**
They buy news stories on a "limited basis, usually on assignment, fee negotiable." Payment for feature stories is "negotiable." They "rarely, if ever, kill a story once assigned. If we sign a contract with a writer, we fulfill it." Advances for expenses are negotiable. Payment is "negotiable — 100% on acceptance or 100% on publication." The payment per photo is "negotiable, depending on use."

# Magazines

## Today's Supervisor
Association Monthly

National Safety Council
1121 Spring Lake Drive
Itasca, IL 60143
708-775-2281

---
**NPayment Information**

Advance paid .................. None    Kill Fee ....See Comments

Expenses paid

........N........ Travel    ........N..... Fax

........N......... Overnight Del.    ........Y...... Phone

---

Payment is 100% on acceptance. No payment for rewrites, updates, syndication or resales; they do pay 25% for reprints.

### Submission Criteria And Policy

Today's Supervisor does not consider unsolicited manuscripts and accepts or rejects an assignment in 2 to 4 weeks. They respond to a query in 2-4 months. They use a written contract and claim all rights.

Today's Supervisor does not accept simultaneous submissions and they do not accept proposals for articles over the telephone.

### Publication Buys Freelance Submissions On...

| Category | Minimum Words | Maximum Words | Minimum Payment | Maximum Payment | Per |
|---|---|---|---|---|---|
| Feature Stories | 800 | 850 |  | $225.00 | Story |

### Advice for Writers:
"Conform to writer's guidelines and angle as closely as possible."

### Editorial Comments:
Sample copies are available. The magazine's field is safety and the most frequently covered topics are safe work practices and occupational-health issues. They pay a kill fee "rarely, we prefer rewrites."

# Magazines

## Vegetarian Times
*Consumer Monthly*

P.O. Box 570
Oak Park, IL 60303
708-848-8100

---

**Payment Information**

Advance paid .................. None    Kill Fee .................. Neg.

Expenses paid

........Y.......... Travel           ........Y....... Fax

........Y.......... Overnight Del.   ........Y...... Phone

---

Payment is 100% on acceptance. No payment for rewrites or updates. They don't have syndication or resales and generally request permission from the author for reprints.

### Submission Criteria And Policy

Vegetarian Times responds to queries sometimes immediately and sometimes no sooner than 4 weeks. "It depends on when it hits the desk." First-time submissions are on spec. They use a written contract and acquire all rights.

Vegetarian Times doesn't accept simultaneous submissions or previously published articles. They accept unsolicited manuscripts, but don't want writers to query by telephone.

### Publication Buys Freelance Submissions On...

| Category | Minimum Words | Maximum Words | Minimum Payment | Maximum Payment | Per |
|---|---|---|---|---|---|
| News | 200 | 800 | $75.00 | $150.00 | Story |
| Feature Stories | 1800 | 3500 | $450.00 | Neg. | Story |
| Book Reviews | 200 | 800 | $75.00 | $150.00 | Story |

# Magazines

**Advice for Writers:**
"Stories should have something to do with vegetarianism, animal rights, environmental issues, or health. They should have a vegetarian angle."

**Editorial Comments:**
Expenses vary and are usually negotiable. Regarding changes to stories, "changes in information are always checked with the author; changes in style rarely are. Galleys may or may not be sent to writers, depending on the circumstances."

# Newspapers

## Windy City Times
Weekly Newspaper for Gays/Lesbians

970 W. Montana
Chicago, IL 60614
312-935-1974

### Payment Information

Advance paid .................. None    Kill Fee .................. 50%

Expenses paid

........N........ Travel           .......N....... Fax

........Y........ Overnight Del.   .......N....... Phone

Payment is 100% on publication. They do not pay for rewrites, and didn't indicate if they pay for syndication, reprints or resales. They do pay for updates.

### Submission Criteria And Policy

Windy City Times considers unsolicited manuscripts, and accepts or rejects an assignment in 1 to 3 weeks. They use a verbal contract and claim one-time rights.

Windy City Times accepts simultaneous submissions. They accept proposals for articles over the telephone.

### Publication Buys Freelance Submissions On...

| Category | Min. Words | Max. Words | Min. Pay. | Max. Pay. | Per | Cont. |
|---|---|---|---|---|---|---|
| News | 400 | 1500 | $25.00 | $50.00 | Story | D. Perreten |
| Feature Stories | 1250 | 2000 | $60.00 | $1000.00 | Story | D. Perreten |
| Opinion Pieces | 1000 | 1500 | | | Story | D. Perreten |

### Editorial Comments:
They do not ask writers to provide photographs.

# Magazines

## Your Money
*Investment Bimonthly Magazine*

Consumer Digest, Inc.
5705 N. Lincoln Ave.
Chicago, IL 60659
312-275-3590

### Payment Information

Advance paid .................. None       Kill Fee .................. 50%

Expenses paid

........N.......... Travel           .......Y...... Fax

........Y.......... Overnight Del.    .......Y....... Phone

Payment is 100% on publication. No payment for rewrites, updates, syndication, reprints or resales.

### Submission Criteria And Policy

Your Money considers unsolicited manuscripts "occasionally." They accept or reject an assignment in 1 week. They use a written contract and acquire various rights.

Your Money does not accept simultaneous submissions. They do not accept proposals for articles over the telephone.

See Comments for other information.

### Publication Buys Freelance Submissions On...

| Category | Min. Words | Max. Words | Min. Pay. | Max. Pay. | Per | Cont. |
|---|---|---|---|---|---|---|
| Departmental | 200 | 500 | | | Word | D. Fertig |
| Feature Stories | 2000 | 2500 | $.25 | $.35 | Word | D. Fertig |

### Advice for Writers:
"Do not send manuscripts; send a briefly outlined proposal for a personal-finance article with a timely twist."

# Magazines

**Editorial Comments:**
They use both a verbal and written contract: the written contract specifies "work for hire;" it also specifies that they pay on acceptance, but the survey states they pay 100% on publication. The contract also stipulates that writers obtain written authorization in advance for any expenses over $50. They do not require writers to provide photographs, but "they are asked to provide real-people examples that can be photographed." The rates for "Departmental & other" were listed as "flat rate" per word.

# Kill Fees

The National Writers Union advocates abolishing the "kill fee," which is given when an editor or publisher commissions a piece from a writer but then decides not to publish it.

Here is a list of some of the kill fees (subject to change) of Chicago-area publications. Kill fees range from a set amount to a percentage of the agreed-upon fee for the article.

The NWU encourages writers to negotiate higher kill fees whenever possible, and to encourage editors to help rid the publishing industry of this abusive practice.

**$50**
Chicago Tribune

**$100-$200**
Chicago Reporter

**20%**
Playboy Magazine
Real Estate Today

**25%**
New City

**30%**
Journal of Property Management

**33%**
Chicago Enterprise
Illinois Medicine

**50%**
Campus Life
Confetti
Inland Architect
North Shore
The Lutheran
Windy City Times
Your Money

**No Kill Fee**

Chicago Life Magazine
Chicago Reader
Christian Century
Crain's Small Business
Crain's Chicago Business
Discovery YMCA
Facets
Fancy Food
Floral & Nursery Times
Fra Noi
Grocery Marketing
Hotels
Illinois Pharmacist
Joliet Herald-News
Law Practice Management
Logan Square Extra
N'Digo
New Art Examiner
News-Sun
Standard Rate & Data
Systems Management 3X

# Payment Policies

Getting paid is one of the headaches of being a freelance writer. The National Writers Union recommends that writers be paid within 30 days of submission of the work.

A number of publications will accept an article but withhold payment until it is published, which can be six months or even a year later. None of the publications in our survey pays on assignment — in other words, before the research, interviewing and writing begins.

Here are some of the payment policies of Chicago-area publications.

### Pays on Submission
Access
Discovery YMCA

### Pays on Acceptance
ABA Journal
Campus Life
Catalyst
Chicago Enterprise
Chicago Reporter
Chicago Tribune
Confetti
Crain's Chicago Business
Crain's Small Business
Electric Light & Power
Facets
Grocery Marketing
Hotels
Illinois Medicine
Illinois Pharmacist
Journal of Property Management
The Lion Magazine
The Lutheran
Marketing News
Playboy Magazine
The Rotarian
Real Estate Today
Safety & Health
Salt
Telephony
Today's Supervisor

### Pays on Publication
Advertising Age
Chicago Life Magazine
Chicago Outlines
Chicago Parent
Chicago Reader
Christian Century
Fancy Food
Floral & Nursery Times
Illinois Legal Times
Illinois Pharmacist
Inland Architect
Law Practice Management
Logan Square Extra
N'Digo
Neighborhood Works
New Art Examiner
New City
News-Sun
Planning Magazine
Stagebill
Standard Rate & Data
Systems Management 3X
Telephony
Windy City Times
Your Money

# Contract Types

Since oral agreements are prone to misinterpretation and forgetfulness, the National Writers Union recommends that writers use a written contract, preferably the NWU Standard Journalism Contract.

With a written contract in hand, it is easier to demand payment (if delayed or denied) and recall other important aspects of the assignment. As the saying goes, "An oral contract isn't worth the paper it's written on."

A contract, of course, should be signed by both writer and editor (or publisher), thereby signifying an agreement between the two parties. For publications not accustomed to using written contracts, the NWU advises members to send the NWU Standard Journalism Contract.

Here are some of the policies of Chicago-area publications.

### No Contract
Chicago Life Magazine
Chicago Reader
Christian Century
Fancy Food
Floral & Nursery Times
Fra Noi
Illinois Pharmacist
Law Practice Management
Logan Square Extra
The Lutheran
News-Sun

### Oral Agreement
Chicago Outlines
Chicago Parent
Chicago Tribune
Confetti
Electric Light & Power
Facets
Grocery Marketing
Hotels
Inland Architect
N'Digo
New Art Examiner
New City
Safety & Health
Stagebill

Standard Rate & Data
Systems Management 3X
Windy City Times

### Written Contract
ABA Journal
Access
Barrister Magazine
Campus Life
Catalyst
Chicago Enterprise
Chicago Reporter
Crain's Chicago Business
Crain's Small Business
Discovery YMCA
Illinois Legal Times
Illinois Medicine
Joliet Herald-News
Journal of Property Management
The Lion Magazine
Marketing News
Neighborhood Works
Planning Magazine
Real Estate Today
The Rotarian
Salt
Telephony
Today's Supervisor

# By THE BOOK

**A Bonus Section on Special Libraries in the Chicago Area**

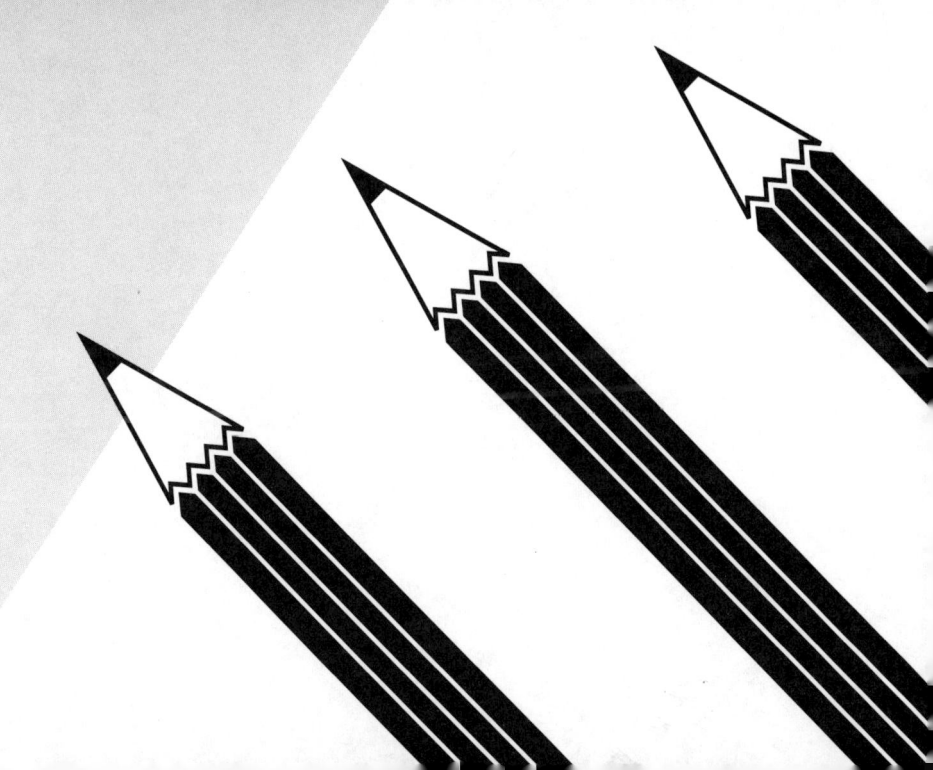

# Special Libraries in the Chicago Area

By LaVaughn Robert Jones, Information Specialist
©1993 Knowledge Tree. All Rights Reserved.

If you're a freelance writer looking for an obscure periodical, a source of funding or a quiet place to do your research, don't despair. The Chicago area is blessed with many special libraries covering a wide range of subjects.

Many are open to serious researchers, but access frequently comes with restrictions. Chiefly, most of these libraries do not allow materials to leave the premises. Outsiders are not granted access to information of a proprietary nature, particularly at association and corporate libraries housing internal research and competitive strategies.

This chapter contains a selective cross-section of libraries providing reference use only access to writers and other researchers. Unless otherwise noted, borrowing privileges are restricted to organization members, although some libraries allow interlibrary lending.

Arranged by main subject categories, the listings include special-use information (when available) and hours. Included are libraries located in colleges and universities, trade and professional associations, corporations, state and federal agencies, museums and other cultural institutions. Particular emphasis is given to special collections.

A couple of notes on recurring terms and names:

■ Government document depositories – Some libraries are identified as U.S. government and state document depositories, which house bills, regulations, reports and treaties. U.S. depositories also carry the records and publications of federal agencies, Congress and the executive branch. Illinois depositories typically include state laws, legislative debates, administrative regulations and periodicals.

■ ERIC – Another name that pops up frequently is the Educational Resources Information Center (part of the U.S. Department of Education). ERIC includes materials on early childhood; handicapped and gifted children; higher education; languages and linguistics; reading and communication skills; teacher education; tests and evaluation. Materials are disseminated largely through the ERIC database and CD-ROM (compact disc-read only memory), available at most college libraries and many public libraries.

This article is not a complete report of every special library, but it should give writers an idea of the depth and breadth of libraries supplementing the public library system. For the most up-to-date information (hours and access rules may change), call specific libraries beforehand.

## Academic and General Collections

BARAT COLLEGE LIBRARY—700 E. Westleigh Road, Lake Forest 60045; (708) 295-4488, fax 615-5000. Subject areas include women's studies. Special collections: 19th-century women's rights periodicals, Roman Catholic theology and philosophy, Middle-English literature. Open Mon.-Thurs. 9 a.m.-10 p.m., Fri. 9 a.m.-5 p.m., Sat. 10 a.m.-5 p.m., Sun. 5 p.m.-9 p.m.

CENTER FOR RESEARCH LIBRARIES—6050 S. Kenwood Ave., Chicago 60637; (312) 955-4545. Special collections include Africana, college catalogs, U.S. and foreign newspapers, U.S. ethnic newspapers, foreign doctoral dissertations, war-crimes documents, children's books, Latin America. A U.S. government document depository. Open Mon.-Fri. 9 a.m.-4:30 p.m.

COLUMBIA COLLEGE LIBRARY—600 S. Michigan Ave., Chicago 60605; (312) 663-1600, ext. 153. Subject areas include art, dance, film, journalism, photography, television, radio, theater, arts-and-entertainment management. Special collections: George Lurie Fine Arts Collection, Black Music Resource Collection. Open Mon.-Thurs. 8 a.m.-9 p.m., Fri. 8 a.m.-6 p.m., Sat. 9 a.m.-5 p.m.; hours subject to change between school sessions.

DePAUL UNIVERSITY LIBRARIES—2350 N. Kenmore Ave. (at Fullerton), Chicago 60614; (312) 362-8066. Special collections: art books, sports, Dickens, Horace, Napoleon, Verrona Derr Collection of African-American Studies. A U.S. government document depository. Open Mon.-Thurs. 8 a.m.-midnight, Fri. 8 a.m.-6 p.m., Sat. 9 a.m.-6 p.m., Sun. noon-midnight; hours subject to change between school sessions.

GOVERNORS STATE UNIVERSITY LIBRARY—Governors Highway and Stuenkel Road, University Park 60466-0975; (708) 534-4111. Subject areas include business, management, economics, education, environmental studies, ethnic studies, health sciences, law. Special collections: art slides, Schomberg Collection of African-American literature, ERIC. A U.S. government and Illinois document depository. Open Mon.-Thurs. 8:30 a.m.-10 p.m.; Fri.-Sat. 8:30 a.m.-5 p.m.; Sun. 5 p.m.-9 p.m.

LAKE FOREST COLLEGE—Donnelly Library, Sheridan and College Roads, Lake Forest 60045-2396; (708) 234-3100, fax 234-7170. Special collections: Scotland, printing history, western Americana, theater, railroads, New York

Daily News. A U.S. and Illinois document depository. Open Mon.-Thurs. 8 a.m.-midnight, Fri. 8 a.m.-10 p.m., Sat. 10 a.m.-10 p.m., Sun. 11:30 a.m.-2 p.m.

WILLIAM RAINEY HARPER COLLEGE—Learning Resource Center, Algonquin and Roselle Roads, Palatine 60067; (708) 397-3000, fax 397-0433. Special collections: U.S. Department of Commerce, legal technology. An Illinois document depository. Open Mon.-Thurs. 8 a.m.-10 p.m., Fri. 8 a.m.-4:30 p.m., Sat. 9 a.m.-3:30 p.m., Sun. 1 p.m.-5 p.m.

LOYOLA UNIVERSITY OF CHICAGO—Elizabeth M. Cudahy Memorial Library, 6525 N. Sheridan Road, Chicago 60626; (312) 508-2641, 508-2993. Subject areas include humanities, philosophy, theology. As a result of a merger, the general science collection is housed at Mundelein College (see listing below). Special collection: Loyola University archives. A U.S. and Illinois document depository. Open Mon.-Fri. 9 a.m.-4 p.m.

MUNDELEIN COLLEGE—Learning Resource Center, 6363 N. Sheridan Road, Chicago 60660; (312) 262-8100. Subject areas include religious studies, social and behavioral sciences, women's studies. Special collections: literature for children and adolescents, textbook and curriculum material. Open Mon.-Fri. 7:30 a.m.-4 p.m. (Due to the Mundelein-Loyola merger, placement of collections is changing; see listing above.)

NATIONAL OPINION RESEARCH CENTER (NORC)—Paul B. Sheatsley Library, University of Chicago, 1155 E. 60th St., Chicago 60637-2667; (312) 753-7679. Subject areas include methodology and substantive applications, population, public-opinion research. Special collections: Gallup and Harris polls, Canadian Gallup, current public-opinion polls for California, CBS and NBC News, New York Times, Los Angeles Times. Open Mon.-Fri. 8:30 a.m.-5 p.m. Since staffing is limited, call beforehand.

NORTHEASTERN ILLINOIS UNIVERSITY—Ronald Williams Library, 5500 N. St. Louis Ave., Chicago 60625-4699; (312) 794-2615, fax 794-2550. Subject areas include anthropology, education, ethnic studies, psychology. Special collections: Chicago and Cook County archives (1831-1955), American prose and fiction (1774-1900), ERIC, U.S. Department of Health, Education and Welfare, League of Nations documents, American and English little magazines. A U.S. and Illinois document depository. Open Mon.-Thurs. 7:45 a.m.-10 p.m., Fri. 7:45 a.m.-6 p.m., Sat. 9 a.m.-5 p.m., Sun. noon-5 p.m.

NORTHWESTERN UNIVERSITY LIBRARY—1935 Sheridan Road, Evanston 60208; (708) 491-7658. Special collections: Africana, Frank Lloyd Wright, contemporary music scores, women's liberation, United Nations documents, General Agreement on Tariffs and Trade, Organization of American States, European

Communities. A U.S. and Illinois documents depository. Open Mon.-Fri. 8:30 a.m.-5 p.m., Sat. 8:30 a.m.-noon.

ROSARY COLLEGE—Rebecca Crown Library, 7900 W. Division St., River Forest 60305-1066; (708) 366-5205, fax 366-8699. Subject areas include library and information science. Special collections: American fiction (1774-1900), 18th- and 19th-century British culture, anti-slavery propaganda, Western Americana. A U.S. government document depository. Open Mon.-Fri. 8 a.m.-10 p.m., Sat. 8:30 a.m.-5 p.m., Sun. 1 p.m.-10 p.m. Users holding a current library card from a member library in the Suburban Library System may borrow materials; others are granted reference use only.

ROOSEVELT UNIVERSITY—Murray-Green Library, 430 S. Michigan Ave., Chicago 60605; (312) 341-3639, fax 341-3655. Special collections: Library Resources Microbook Collection of American Civilization and English Literature; collection of books, sheet music, recordings; children's books. Open Mon.-Thurs. 9 a.m.-9 p.m., Fri. 9 a.m.-5 p.m., Sat. 11 a.m.-4 p.m.

SAINT XAVIER COLLEGE—Byrne Memorial Library, 3700 W. 103rd, Chicago 60655; (312) 779-3300, fax 779-5231. Subject areas include business, education, nursing, religious studies. Open Mon.-Fri. 7:45 a.m.-10 p.m.; Sat. 8 a.m.-6 p.m.

THEATRE HISTORICAL SOCIETY OF AMERICA—Archive and Research Center, 152 N. York Road #200, Elmhurst 60126; (708) 782-1800. Special collections: blueprints, Chicago Architectural Photographing Company, Bill Clifford, Ben Hall, Terry Helgesen, Bill Peterson, post cards, slides, theater listings, negatives, videotapes. Open by appointment only; please write or call for an appointment two weeks in advance.

UNIVERSITY OF ILLINOIS at CHICAGO—University Library, 801 S. Morgan St., P.O. Box 8198, Chicago 60680; (312) 996-2716, fax 413-0424. Subject areas include art and architecture, business, management, economics, engineering, ethnic studies, humanities, science, technology, social and behavioral sciences. Special collections: Chicago design, Board of Trade, Chicago fairs and expos, Chicagoana, Midwest women's history, Chicago literature and literary societies, Chicago Urban League, sheet music, Franklin Delano Roosevelt. A U.S. and Illinois document depository. Open Mon.-Thurs. 7:30 a.m.-10 p.m., Fri. 7:30 a.m.-7 p.m., Sat. 10 a.m.-5 p.m., Sun. 1 p.m.-9 p.m. Reference service provided Mon.-Thurs. 9 a.m.-6 p.m., Fri. 9 a.m.-4:45 p.m., Sat. 10 a.m.-4:45 p.m.

WHEATON COLLEGE—Buswell Memorial Library, 510 College Ave. Wheaton 60187; (708) 752-5194. Subject areas: American and English literature, anthropology, history, philosophy, political science, religion. Special collections:

Samuel Johnson, Dickens, John Bunyan, Madeline L'Engle. A U.S. government document depository. Open Mon.-Fri. 8 a.m.-9:45 p.m.; Sat. 9 a.m.-5 p.m.

## Art and Design

AMERICAN FLORAL ART SCHOOL LIBRARY—39 S. Wabash, Chicago 60605; (312) 922-9328. Subject areas include floral arrangement, design, symbolism. Open by appointment only.

ART INSTITUTE OF CHICAGO—Ryerson and Burnham Libraries, S. Michigan Ave. at Adams, Chicago 60603; (312) 443-3666. Special collections: 18th- and 19th-century architecture, Midwestern architecture, Chicago art and artists scrapbooks, newspapers (1890 to date), Russian art, archives, photographic collections. Open for one-time reference use by non-members residing in Chicago area with an Infopass from a public library. Potential users who do not live in the area may use the library after presenting proof of residency.

SCHOOL OF THE ART INSTITUTE OF CHICAGO—John M. Flaxman Library, 37 S. Wabash, 6th Floor, Chicago 60603; (312) 899-5097. Subject areas include art, photography, film, humanities, education, music. Special collections: Joan Flasch artists' books, film study collection. Open Mon.-Fri. 8:30 a.m.-9 p.m.; Sat. 10 a.m.-4 p.m.; hours subject to change between school sessions.

HARRINGTON INSTITUTE OF INTERIOR DESIGN LIBRARY—410 S. Michigan Ave., Chicago 60605; (312) 939-4975. Subject areas include architecture, design, furniture. Special collections: current catalogs of contemporary furnishings, paint color catalogs, plastic-laminate samples. Open by appointment only; referral from another library is required.

MUSEUM OF CONTEMPORARY ART LIBRARY—237 E. Ontario St., Chicago 60611; (312) 280-2692. Special collections: artists' books, color slides, photographs, catalogs, brochures, clippings on individual artists and institutions, videotapes and audiotapes of artists discussing their work. Open by appointment only.

## Biological Sciences
*See also Environment, Science and Technology*

CHICAGO BOTANIC GARDEN LIBRARY—Box 400, Glencoe 60022; (708) 835-5440, fax 835-4484. Located on Lake Cook Road a half-mile east of U.S. Hwy. 41. Subject areas include horticulture, botany, agriculture and nature studies. Open Mon.-Sat. 9 a.m.-4 p.m.

CHICAGO ZOOLOGICAL SOCIETY LIBRARY—8400 W. 31st St., Brookfield 60513; (708) 485-0263. Subject areas include natural history, animal behavior and zoology. Open to the public with restrictions: the library prefers telephone and written queries to determine if access is needed; if so, an appointment is then set.

FIELD MUSEUM OF NATURAL HISTORY LIBRARY—Roosevelt Road and Lake Shore Drive, Chicago 60605. (312) 922-9410, fax 427-7269. Subject areas include anthropology, botany, geology, paleontology, zoology, as well as science/engineering. Special collections: Ayer Ornithology Library, Laufer Collection of Far Eastern Studies, Schmidt Herpetology Library. A U.S. government document depository. Open Mon.-Fri. 8:30 a.m.-4:30 p.m.

LINCOLN PARK ZOOLOGICAL GARDENS LIBRARY—2200 N. Cannon Drive, Chicago 60614; (312) 294-4640. Subject areas include zoology, animal behavior and care, wildlife conservation, management of captive wild animals, endangered species and zoos. Special collections: posters, Marlin Perkins videotapes, Zoo and Animal Reference Collection, which contains information on nearly 200 zoos and aquariums. Open by appointment only.

MORTON ARBORETUM—STERLING MORTON LIBRARY, Lisle 60532; (708) 719-2427 or 719-2430. Subject areas include botany, horticulture, dendrology, arboriculture, landscape architecture, natural history, ecology, environment. Special collections: rare books in botany and horticulture; nursery and seed catalogs; landscape architecture; botanical prints and drawings; maps of the arboretum. Open Mon.-Fri. 9 a.m.-5 p.m., Sat. 10 a.m.-4 p.m.

JOHN G. SHEDD AQUARIUM LIBRARY—1200 S. Lake Shore Drive, Chicago 60605; (312) 939-2426, ext. 2289. Subject areas include animals, aquaculture, aquariums, aquatic plants, Great Lakes, marine ecology, water pollution. Open Wed.-Sat. 1 p.m.-5 p.m.

## Business and Finance

AMERICAN COLLEGE OF HEALTHCARE EXECUTIVES—Richard J. Stull Memorial Learning Resources Center, 840 N. Lake Shore Drive, Chicago 60611; (312) 943-0544. Subject areas include health-services administration and management. Open by appointment only.

AMERICAN FEDERATION OF SMALL BUSINESS INFORMATION CENTER—407 S. Dearborn St. #500, Chicago 60605; (312) 427-0207. Subject areas include small business, economic education, federal and state legislation, labor laws. Special collections: Soviet imperialism, union power vs. right-to-work. Open by appointment only with restrictions.

AMERICAN MARKETING ASSOCIATION—MARGUERITE KENT LIBRARY AND INFORMATION CENTER, 250 S. Wacker Drive, Chicago 60606; (312) 648-0536. Special collections: complete issue runs of Journal of Marketing, Journal of Health Care Marketing, Journal of Marketing Research, Marketing News and all other association publications. Open by appointment only. A $25 fee per visit is charged to non-members.

AMOCO CORPORATION LIBRARY AND INFORMATION CENTER—200 E. Randolph St., Chicago 60601; (312) 856-5961. Subject areas include petroleum technology, business, law, chemistry, engineering. Open by appointment only.

CHICAGO BOARD OF TRADE LIBRARY—141 W. Jackson, Chicago 60604; (312) 435-3552. Subject areas include commodity exchanges, futures trading, financial instruments, agricultural economics, options, business and finance. Special collections: statistical annuals of the Board of Trade (1858 to present), futures and Treasury bills (1956 to present), government reports, newsletters. Open Mon.-Fri. 1:30 p.m.-5 p.m.

CHICAGO MERCANTILE EXCHANGE LIBRARY AND RESOURCE CENTER—30 S. Wacker Drive, Chicago 60606; (312) 930-8239. Subject areas include commodity futures trading. Publishes Index to Day Clips, a special online index. Open Mon.-Fri. 7 a.m.-4:45 p.m.

CHICAGO TRIBUNE MARKETING INFORMATION CENTER—435 N. Michigan Ave., 2nd Floor, Chicago 60611; (312) 222-3188, fax 222-3935. Subject areas include advertising, retailing, market research, newspapers, competing media. Open by appointment only.

FEDERAL RESERVE BANK OF CHICAGO LIBRARY—230 S. LaSalle St., Chicago 60604; (312) 322-5828. Subject areas include agricultural economics, business conditions, central banking economics, finance, monetary policy, statistics. Open Mon.-Fri. 9 a.m.-4:30 p.m.

FIRST NATIONAL BANK OF CHICAGO CORPORATE INFORMATION CENTER—One First National Plaza, Chicago 60670-0477; (312) 732-4000. Subject areas include banking, economics, finance, industry. Open by appointment only with restrictions.

KEMPER GROUP HUMAN RESOURCES INFORMATION CENTER—Route 22 and Kemper Road, Long Grove 60049; (708) 540-2229. Subjects include insurance law, general law, insurance. Open by appointment only.

KPMG PEAT MARWICK INFORMATION AND RESEARCH CENTER—303 E. Wacker Drive, Chicago 60601; (312) 938-1000, fax 938-0449. Subject areas include accounting and auditing, business and management consulting. Open by appointment only, with restrictions.

LOYOLA UNIVERSITY OF CHICAGO—Julia Deal Lewis Library, Lewis Towers, 820 N. Michigan Ave. Chicago 60611-2196; (312) 965-6622, 915-6515. Subject areas include business administration, education. A U.S. and Illinois document depository. Open Mon.-Fri. 7:30 a.m.-9:30 p.m., Sat. 8:30 a.m.-5 p.m.

NATIONAL ASSOCIATION OF REALTORS LIBRARY—430 N. Michigan Ave., Chicago 60611-4087; (312) 329-8292. Subject areas include real estate. Publishes Real Estate Index. Open Mon.-Fri. 9 a.m.-5 p.m. A $25 fee per visit is charged to non-members.

NORTHWESTERN UNIVERSITY, CHICAGO—Joseph Schaffner Library, Graduate School of Management and University College, 339 E. Chicago Ave., Chicago 60611; (312) 503-8422. Subject areas include business, humanities, social sciences. A U.S. and Illinois document depository. Open Mon.-Thurs. noon-10 p.m., Fri. 9 a.m.-5 p.m., Sat. noon-5 p.m.

## Education
*See also Academic and General Collections*

CENTER LIBRARY—(Formerly the Northwest Educational Cooperative Library) 1855 Mount Prospect Road, Des Plaines 60018; (708) 803-3535. Subject areas include bilingual education, educational improvements, English as a second language, literacy, refugee assistance, special education, vocational education. Open by appointment only.

## Energy
*See also Science and Technology*

AMERICAN NUCLEAR SOCIETY LIBRARY—555 N. Kensington Ave., La Grange Park 60525; (708) 352-6611, fax 352-6464. Subject areas include nuclear science and engineering, business management, science biographies. Open Mon.-Fri. 9 a.m.-2 p.m., with restrictions.

AMOCO CORPORATION CENTRAL RESEARCH LIBRARY—Amoco Research Center, 10 Box 400, Naperville 60566; (708) 420-5545, fax 961-7992. Subject areas include petroleum chemistry, physics, engineering, chemistry, chemical engineering, economics, polymers. Special collections: U.S. chemical patents on microfilm (1970 to the present). Open by appointment only with restrictions.

INSTITUTE OF GAS TECHNOLOGY TECHNICAL INFORMATION CENTER—3424 S. State St., Chicago 60616; (312) 567-3963, fax 567-5209. Subject areas include natural-gas technology, energy, coal, bioengineering, chemical engineering. Special collections: American Chemical Society Division of Fuel Chemistry Preprints; Pipeline Simulation Interest Group papers; industrial, organizational and governmental reports; dissertations; Congressional hearings; patents. Open by appointment only.

PEOPLES GAS LIGHT & COKE CO. LIBRARY—122 S. Michigan #727, Chicago 60603; (312) 431-4677, fax 431-4120. Subject areas include business, management, energy, Illinois, public utilities. Special collections: American Gas Association Proceedings (Operating Section), National Association of Regulatory Utility Commissioners, Conference Board publications, federal reports, Edison Electrical Institute proceedings. Open by appointment only.

## Environment
*See also Biological Sciences, Science and Technology*

ENVIRONMENTAL PROTECTION AGENCY—Region V Library, 230 S. Dearborn St., #1670, Chicago 60604; (312) 353-2022. Subject areas include pollution, environmental law, Great Lakes area, hazardous waste, noise, radiation, solid-waste management, toxic waste, water supply and quality. Special collection: air pollution. Open Mon.-Fri. 8 a.m.-5 p.m.

METROPOLITAN WATER RECLAMATION DISTRICT OF GREATER CHICAGO LIBRARY—100 E. Erie St., 5th Floor, Chicago 60611; (312) 751-5782, 751-5813. Subject areas include environmental studies and waste-water treatment. Special collections include reports and proceedings of the Reclamation District, Metropolitan Sanitary District and other predecessors. Open Mon.-Fri. 9 a.m.-4 p.m.

NORTHEASTERN ILLINOIS PLANNING COMMISSION (NIPC) LIBRARY—400 W. Madison St., Chicago 60606-2642; (312) 454-0400. Subject areas include environmental studies, Chicago-area demographic data. Special collections: NIPC publications, data bulletins, energy data, forecasts, housing reports, local assistance, planning aids, policy plans, recreation information, transportation reports, water quality. In addition, the library has selected printouts of U.S. Census summary tapes and socioeconomic data for Northeastern Illinois. A U.S., Illinois and Cook County document depository.

## Ethnic

BALZEKAS MUSEUM OF LITHUANIAN CULTURE REFERENCE AND RESEARCH LIBRARY—6500 S. Pulaski Road, Chicago 60629; (312) 582-6500. Subject areas include Lithuanian armor, heraldry, history and culture.

Special collections: art archives, personality and photography archives, Lithuanian genealogy. Open Sun.-Thurs., Sat. 10 a.m.-4 p.m., Fri. 10 a.m.-8 p.m.

CHICAGO PUBLIC LIBRARY: Carter G. Woodson Regional Library, Vivian G. Hirsch Research Collection of Afro-American History and Literature, 9525 S. Halsted, Chicago 60628; (312) 881-6910. Subject areas include Afro-American history, religion, sociology, art, literature and music. Special collections: Illinois Writers Project, Heritage Press Archives, Carl Sang collection of Afro-American history, Charlemae Hill Rollins collection of children's literature, David P. Ross collection of reprints in Afro-Americana and Americana, Horace Revells Cayton Collection. Open Mon.-Thurs. 10 a.m.-8 p.m.; Fri.-Sat. 9 a.m.-5 p.m.

FIELD MUSEUM OF NATURAL HISTORY—Webber Resource Center, Roosevelt Road and Lake Shore Drive, Chicago 60605; (312) 922-9410. Subject areas include North and South American culture and history, archaeology, contemporary Native American issues. Special collections: Nearly 100 videos on American Indian culture that can be viewed in booths at the center. Open daily 10 a.m.-4:30 p.m. Adult admission is $4 except Thursdays (free).

GOETHE INSTITUTE CHICAGO—German Cultural Center Library, 401 N. Michigan, Ground Floor, Chicago 60611; (312) 329-0915, fax 329-2487. Subject areas include German literature, cinema and politics; information guides on German genealogy. Open Wed. and Fri. noon-6 p.m., Thurs. noon-8 p.m., Sat. 10 a.m.-3 p.m.

MITCHELL INDIAN MUSEUM—Kendall College Library, 2408 Orrington Ave., Evanston 60201; (708) 866-1395. North American collection. Open Mon.-Thurs. 9 a.m.-4 p.m.

LITHUANIAN RESEARCH AND STUDIES CENTER—5620 S. Claremont Ave. Chicago 60636-1039; (312) 434-4545. Special collections: cartography, Lithuanian Historical Society, Lithuanian Institute of Education, World Lithuanian archives and community collection.

POLISH MUSEUM OF AMERICA LIBRARY—984 N. Milwaukee Ave., Chicago 60622; (312) 384-3352, fax 278-4585. Special collections: literary works (16th-17th centuries), royal manuscripts (16th-18th centuries), original manuscripts of Polish statesmen and patriots (Kosciuszko, Pulaski, Paderewski), plus newspapers, magazines, Polish publishers in U.S., 19th-century emigrés, oral history. Open Mon.-Sat. 10 a.m.-4 p.m.

SWEDISH-AMERICAN HISTORICAL SOCIETY—5125 N. Spaulding Ave., Chicago 60625; (312) 583-5722. Subject areas include settlement in U.S. and Swedish culture. Special collections include contributions of Swedes to U.S. life and culture, Swedish organizations in the U.S., music, royalty. Open by appointment only; offers translation services.

# History

CHICAGO HISTORICAL SOCIETY RESEARCH COLLECTIONS—Clark Street and North Avenue, Chicago 60614-6099; (312) 642-4600. Subject areas include Chicago, Civil War, Illinois, Abraham Lincoln, U.S. history to 1865. Special collections: Chicago City Directories (1839-1929), archives and manuscripts, architecture, prints and photographs, periodicals. Open Mon.-Sat. 9:30 a.m.-4:30 p.m. Library users do not have to pay an admission fee to use the library, but users must sign in at the front desk and receive a pass. To use certain collections (e.g., prints and photographs), an appointment must be made. Generally, it is best to make such appointments in person.

CHICAGO MUNICIPAL REFERENCE LIBRARY—Government Publications Department of Chicago Public Library's Harold Washington Library Center, 400 S. State, 5th Floor, Chicago 60605; (312) 747-4500. Subject areas include all aspects of Chicago, city planning, criminology, housing, personnel, public administration and financing, urban studies. Special collections: newspaper clippings, government documents, community-area information, street names, political campaigns. (This library was formerly located in City Hall.)

NATIONAL WOMEN'S CHRISTIAN TEMPERANCE UNION—Frances E. Willard Memorial Library, 1730 Chicago Ave., Evanston 60201; (708) 864-1396, ext. 16. Subject areas include alcohol, drugs, prohibition history, social and behavioral sciences, temperance, tobacco and related subjects, women's history. Open Mon.-Thurs. 9 a.m.-noon and 1 p.m.-2:30 p.m.

NEWBERRY LIBRARY—60 W. Walton St., Chicago 60610-3394; (312) 943-9090. Subject areas include U.S. history and literature to 1900, Civil War and anti-slavery, Arthuriana, art of war before 1890. Also includes calligraphy, European history and literature (1300-1900), genealogy and heraldry, history of cartography and Latin American history and literature to 1920. Special collections: American Indian culture, discovery and colonization, Americana and the West, history of printing, Sherwood Anderson papers, Herman Melville Collection. Open Tues.-Thurs. 10 a.m.-6 p.m., Fri.-Sat. 9 p.m.-5 p.m.

THE SHAKESPEARE DATA BANK—1217 Ashland Ave., Evanston 60202; (708) 475-7550. A private collection of more than 8,000 works by and about Shakespeare and his time, noteworthy for its comprehensiveness and its continual acquisition of new materials. Questions should be directed to Louis Marder.

# Law

ALLSTATE INSURANCE CORPORATE LIBRARY—E5 Allstate Plaza, Northbrook 60062; (708) 402-5407, 402-6014. Subjects: insurance and law. Open by appointment only.

COOK COUNTY LAW LIBRARY—2900 Richard J. Daley Center, Chicago 60602; (312) 443-5423, fax 332-7814. Subject areas include Anglo-American and foreign law. A U.S. and Illinois government documents depository with seven branches. Open Mon.- Fri. 2 p.m.-9 p.m. (main library). Branch libraries are generally open Mon.-Fri. 8:30 a.m.-4 p.m.; call specific branches for details: Bridgeview (708) 974-6201, Criminal Court (312) 890-7100, Michigan Avenue (312) 341-2765, Markham (708) 210-4125, Maywood (708) 865-6020, Rolling Meadows (708) 818-2290, Skokie (708) 470-7298.

DEPAUL UNIVERSITY LAW LIBRARY—25 E. Jackson, 7th Floor, Chicago 60604-2287; (312) 362-8121, fax 362-6908. Special collections: Constitutional law, environmental law, graduate health law, graduate taxation law, Illinois municipal codes. A U.S. government document depository. Open Mon.-Fri. 8 p.m.-5 p.m.; Sat. 9 a.m.-6 p.m.; hours subject to change between school sessions.

IIT CHICAGO-KENT COLLEGE OF LAW LIBRARY—77 S. Wacker Drive, Chicago 60606; (312) 567-5014, fax 372-0895. Special collections in international relations, law and business. A U.S. government document depository. Open Mon.-Fri. 9 a.m.-5 p.m.; hours subject to change between school sessions.

NORTHWESTERN UNIVERSITY, CHICAGO—School of Law Library, 357 E. Chicago Ave., Chicago 60611; (312) 503-8451, fax 908-9230. Special collection of international law. Open Mon.-Thurs. 7:30 a.m.-midnight, Fri. 7:30 a.m.-8 p.m., Sat. 9 a.m.-8 p.m., Sun. 9 a.m.-midnight. A U.S. and Illinois government document depository; hours subject to change between school sessions.

UNIVERSITY OF CHICAGO—D'Angelo Law Library, 1121 E. 60th St., Chicago 60637-2786; (312) 702-9615, fax 702-0730. Subject areas include Anglo-American, civil, international law. Special collections: Karl Llewelyn and Henry Simon papers, U.S. Supreme Court records and briefs. A U.S. government document depository. Open Mon.-Fri. 8:30 a.m.-5 p.m.

WILLIAM J. CAMPBELL LIBRARY OF THE U.S. COURTS—219 S. Dearborn St. #1448, Chicago 60604-1769, (312) 435-5660. Subject areas include government publications, federal and state laws (Illinois, Indiana, Wisconsin). A U.S. government document depository. Open Mon.-Fri. 8:30 a.m.-5 p.m.

## Medical

ALZHEIMER'S ASSOCIATION—919 N. Michigan #1000, Chicago 60611-1676; (312) 335-9602. Subjects include Alzheimer's Disease, aging, gerontology. Open Mon.-Fri. 8:30 a.m.-5 p.m.

AMERICAN COLLEGE OF SURGEONS LIBRARY—55 E. Erie St., Chicago 60611; (312) 664-4050. Subject areas include the history of medicine and surgery. Special collection include pamphlets, archival material and surgical films. Open by appointment only.

AMERICAN ACADEMY OF PEDIATRICS—Baldwin Library, 141 Northwest Point Blvd., Elk Grove Village 60009-0927; (708) 981-4722, fax 228-5097. Subject areas include Academy policy and health-care advocacy for children. Open by appointment only.

AMERICAN DENTAL ASSOCIATION—Bureau of Library Services, 211 E. Chicago Ave., Chicago 60611; (312) 440-2653. Special collection: Archives of the American Dental Association. Publishes Index to Dental Literature. Open Mon.-Fri. 8:30 a.m.-5 p.m.

AMERICAN HOSPITAL ASSOCIATION RESOURCE CENTER—840 N. Lake Shore Drive, Chicago 60611; (312) 280-6263, fax 280-3061. Subject areas include hospitals and health-care institutions, administration, planning and financing. Special collections: Ray E. Brown Management Collection, Center for Hospital and Health Care Administration History. Open Mon.-Fri. 8:30 a.m.-4:30 p.m.

AMERICAN MEDICAL ASSOCIATION—Division of Library and Information Management, 515 N. State St., Chicago 60610, (312) 464-4818. Special collections: medical history and artifacts; deceased physician masterfile; economics, sociology and politics of medicine; history of AMA, films, journals, records; unproven (quackery) medical practices. Open to non-members by appointment only.

DEPARTMENT OF VETERANS AFFAIRS MEDICAL CENTER LIBRARY— 3001 N. Green Bay Road, North Chicago 60064; (708) 578-3757. Subjects: medicine, psychiatry, psychology, rehabilitation, social work. Open on a limited basis; phone first. No public photocopy machine is available so users must take notes.

DR. WILLIAM M. SCHOLL COLLEGE OF PODIATRIC MEDICINE LIBRARY—1001 Dearborn St., Chicago 60610; (312) 280-2891. Special collections: historic books, shoes, vintage podiatric instruments. Open Mon.-Thurs. 8 a.m.-11 p.m., Fri. 8 a.m.-6 p.m., Sun. noon-10 p.m.

DuPAGE COUNTY HEALTH DEPARTMENT—John P. Case Library, 111 N. County Farm Road, Wheaton 60187; (708) 682-7400. Subjects: environmental, mental, public health. Open Mon.-Fri. 8 p.m.-4:30 p.m. for reference use only.

ILLINOIS COLLEGE OF OPTOMETRY—Carl F. Shepard Memorial Library, 3241 S. Michigan Ave., Chicago 60616; (312) 225-1700, fax 791-1970. Subject areas include health sciences, medicine, natural science, ophthalmology, optometry, optics, perception. Open Mon.-Fri. 8 a.m..-11 p.m.., Sat.-Sun. 10 a.m.-11 p.m.

LOYOLA UNIVERSITY OF CHICAGO—Medical Center Library, 2160 S. First Ave., Maywood 60153-5585; (708) 216-9192, fax 216-8115. Subject areas include dentistry, health science, medicine, nursing. Open Mon.-Fri. 7:45 a.m.-5 p.m. for reference use only.

MERCY CENTER FOR HEALTH CARE SERVICES—Medical Library, 1325 N. Highland Ave., Aurora 60506; (708) 801-2686. Subject areas include medicine, gerontology, hospital administration, nursing, psychiatry. Open Mon.-Fri. 8 a.m.-4:30 p.m.

NATIONAL SOCIETY TO PREVENT BLINDNESS—Conrad Berens Library, 500 E. Remington Road, Schaumburg 60173; (708) 843-2020. Subject areas include eye health, pathology, preventive medicine. Open Mon.-Fri. 8 a.m.-5 p.m.

RUSH UNIVERSITY LIBRARY—600 S. Paulina St., Chicago 60612-3874; (312) 942-2271, 942-5950. Special collections: medical Americana; local and regional medical imprints, cholera, Dr. Benjamin Rush Collection. Open Mon.-Thurs. 7 a.m.-midnight; Fri. 7 a.m.-6 p.m.; Sat. 9 a.m.-6 p.m.; Sun. 1 p.m.-midnight.

UNIVERSITY OF ILLINOIS AT CHICAGO—Library of the Health Sciences, 1750 Polk St., P.O. Box 7509, Chicago 60680; (312) 996-8974, fax 733-6440. Subject areas include allied health, dentistry, environmental studies, medicine, nursing, pharmacy. Special collections: neurology and psychiatry, urology and anomalies. Open Mon.-Thurs. 7 a.m.-midnight, Fri. 7:30 a.m.-7 p.m., Sat. 8:30 a.m.-5 p.m., Sun. 1:30 p.m.-midnight. Reference service provided Mon.-Fri. 8:30 a.m.-6 p.m.

## Philanthropy

DONORS FORUM OF CHICAGO LIBRARY—53 W. Jackson #430, Chicago 60604; (312) 431-0264. Special collection: philanthropy and private funding. Directories of foundations, grants lists and giving guidelines. Videos about nonprofit organizations, grant-making and fund-raising. Free orientation session begins at 10 a.m. every Tuesday; reservations required.

## Religion

CHICAGO THEOLOGICAL SEMINARY—Hammond Library, 5757 S. University Ave., Chicago 60637; (312) 752-5757. Subject areas include biblical studies, the Black Church, Congregational Church History, religious education materials. Affiliated with the United Church of Christ. Open by appointment only.

CONCORDIA UNIVERSITY—Klinck Memorial Library, 7400 Augusta St.,

Skokie 60305-1499; (708) 209-3050, fax 209-3175. Subject areas include education, music and religious studies. Special collections: curriculum library, complete writings of Martin Luther, ERIC, oral history. Open Sun. 9 a.m.-11 p.m., Mon.-Thurs. 8 a.m.-11 p.m., Fri. 8 a.m.-5 p.m., Sat. 9 a.m.-5 p.m. Users holding a current card for the Suburban Library System may borrow materials; others are granted reference use only. Supported by the Lutheran Church, Missouri Synod.

GARRETT-EVANGELICAL AND SEABURY-WESTERN THEOLOGICAL SEMINARIES—The United Library, 2121-22 Sheridan Road, Evanston 60201; (708) 866-3909 (Garrett); (708) 866-3899 (Seabury). Subject areas include Anglicana, biblical studies, church history, Methodistica, religious-education curriculum, theology, Wesleyana. Special collections: historical materials of the Methodist Church in England and the U.S., the Paul Edwin Keene Bible Collection, Patristic Collection of monographs about church fathers, Egyptology. Open Mon.-Thurs. 8:30 a.m.-10 p.m., Fri. 8:30 a.m.-5 p.m., Sat. 2 p.m.-5 p.m., Sun. 7 p.m.-10 p.m. Affiliated with the United Methodist Church.

HEBREW THEOLOGICAL COLLEGE—Saul Silber Memorial Library, 7135 N. Carpenter Road, Skokie 60077-3263; (708) 674-7750, fax 679-1487. Subject areas include biblical studies, Hebrew literature and Jewish history. Special collections: Holocaust Collection and Women in Judaism. Open Sun. 9:30 a.m.-12:30 p.m., Mon. 9 a.m.-5 p.m., Tues. 12:30 p.m.-5 p.m., Wed.-Thurs. 9 a.m.-5 p.m.

ILLINOIS BENEDICTINE COLLEGE—Theodore Lownik Library, 5700 College Road, Lisle 60532-0900; (708) 960-1500, ext. 8500, fax 960-1126. Special collections: Abraham Lincoln, Catholic theology, Czech heritage. A U.S. and Illinois government document depository. Open Sun. 2 p.m.-11 p.m., Mon.-Thurs. 8:30 a.m.-11 p.m., Fri.-Sat. 9 a.m.-5 p.m. Supported by the Roman Catholic Benedictine Monks of St. Procopius Abbey.

## Science and Technology

ADLER PLANETARIUM LIBRARY—1300 S. Lake Shore Drive, Chicago 60605; (312) 322-0593, fax 322-2257. Subject areas include archaeo-astronomy, astronomy, astrophysics, space research. Special collections: history of astronomy, history of navigation and scientific instruments, maps and atlases in astronomy, charts and globes. Open by appointment only.

ARGONNE NATIONAL LABORATORY—Technical Information Services Department, 9700 S. Cass Ave., Building 203-D140, Argonne 60439-4801; (708) 252-1275. Subject areas include biological sciences, chemical engineering, engineering, environmental science, high-energy physics, mathematical science, medicine, nuclear science, physics. Special collection: technical reports from the

Department of Energy and related agencies. Open by appointment only with restrictions. The library provides only photocopy services to outside users, so phone ahead to ask if specific items are housed by the library. No further reference service is available to those not connected to Argonne.

CHICAGO ACADEMY OF SCIENCES—Matthew Laughlin Memorial Library, Lincoln Park, 2001 N. Clark St., Chicago 60614; (312) 549-0606, 871-2668. Subject areas include environmental studies, geology, ornithology, natural history. Open by appointment only.

ILLINOIS INSTITUTE OF TECHNOLOGY—Paul V. Galvin Library, 35 W. 33rd St., Chicago 60616; (312) 567-6844, fax 567-3955. Subject areas include architecture and design, business, management, computer science, economics, environmental studies, math, science and technology. This library is a U.S. government document depository. Open Mon.-Thurs. 8:30 a.m.-10 p.m., Fri.-Sat. 8:30 a.m.-5 p.m., Sun. 2 p.m.-10 p.m.

MUSEUM OF SCIENCE AND INDUSTRY LIBRARY—57th St. and Lake Shore Drive, Chicago 60637; (312) 684-1414, ext. 2449, fax 684-5580. Subject areas include children's science literature, industrial history, international expositions, science education. Special collections: early autos, microcomputers, aviation, railroading, ships, museology. Open Mon.-Fri. 9:30 a.m.-4 p.m. Adults pay $5 admission except Thursdays (free).

SEARLE RESEARCH LIBRARY—4901 Searle Parkway, Skokie 60077; (708) 982-8285, 982-8095. Subject areas include biology, cardiovascular medicine, chemistry, gastroenterology, gynecology, medicine, pharmacy, pharmacology, toxicology. Open by appointment only.

SIEMENS GAMMASONICS RESEARCH LIBRARY—2501 N. Barrington Road, Hoffman Estates 60195-7372; (708) 390-1989. Subject areas include computer math, digital angiography, gamma cameras, nuclear medical instruments, nuclear physics, scintillation cameras, tomography. Open by appointment. The library follows federal guidelines limiting access to people 18 years and older (due to radioactive materials used in the production of imaging equipment). Interlibrary loan requests are honored for circulating materials.

UNIVERSITY OF CHICAGO—John Crerar Library, 5730 S. Ellis Ave., Chicago 60637-1434; (312) 702-7715, fax 702-3022. Subject areas include astronomy, astrophysics, biological sciences, chemical technology, clinical medicine, engineering, geophysical sciences, history of medicine and science, physics, technology. Special collection: records of the Atomic Scientists' Movement. Open daily 8:30 a.m.-1 a.m.; hours change between school sessions.

USG CORPORATION RESEARCH CENTER LIBRARY—700 N. Highway 45, Libertyville 60048; (708) 362-9797, ext. 520. Subject areas include acoustical products, building materials, cement and cement board, chemistry, construction systems, fibers, fillers, insulation, lime, paper and wood fiber, plaster and wallboard, tooling and casting. Special collection: gypsum rocks. Open on a limited-access basis; the library prefers phone queries to visits. Access is obtained only upon referral from a public library. If a visit becomes necessary, reference appointments must be made at least two days in advance.

## Transportation

CHICAGO TRANSIT AUTHORITY—Anthony Memorial Library, Merchandise Mart Plaza, P.O. Box 3555, Chicago 60654; (312) 664-7200. Subjects include urban transportation. Open by appointment only.

*LaVaughn Robert Jones is an information specialist. His company, Knowledge Tree, provides library and online database research services to individuals and small businesses. Before founding Knowledge Tree, he held information-specialist positions at The Chicago Tribune, DePaul University College of Law and Quaker Oats Company. He is a graduate of the School of Library and Information Science at the University of Illinois at Urbana-Champaign.*

# By WRITERS

## An Inside Look at Top Chicago-Area Publications

# Introduction

*By Keith Watson*

To supplement the information in our listings, we asked several National Writers Union members to interview freelancers and assemble brief reports on what it's like to write for some of the better-known publications in the region. The periodicals in this section include *Chicago* magazine, *The Reader*, the city's two major daily newspapers — the *Chicago Sun-Times* and the *Chicago Tribune* — as well as *Advertising Age* and other Crain business publications. We also include a rundown on *In These Times*, a national biweekly newsmagazine known for being pro-labor.

If you have a relaxed temperament, a good deal of self-discipline and confidence, freelancing can bring much pleasure. You set your own hours, interview interesting people and express yourself. Bylines can strengthen your self-esteem. The anticipated feelings of freedom are why so many people dream of going freelance.

But most writers — particularly those with children — know that it's almost impossible to support oneself on income from freelance journalism alone. A recurring theme in the following collection of short essays — as well as in our survey listings and some of the longer essays in the first section of our book — is the many hours that freelancers must invest upfront to study publications, court editors and obtain assignments — all of which go unpaid. Some publications, such as *The Reader*, expect freelancers, even experienced journalists, to write articles on speculation ("on spec"), meaning that the publication bears no financial obligation to print or pay for any part of the article or for the hours of research involved. Magazines such as *Chicago* seem to pay comparatively well but use contracts with a 25 percent "kill fee," which can result in a writer being paid only a quarter of the agreed-upon fee if the magazine decides his or her piece is "unusable."

In addition, few magazines pay for rewrites or updates, even if necessitated by publishing delays, advertising slumps or an editor's changing demands. The ultimate insult, however, can happen when — after weeks of research, writing and rewriting — getting paid becomes an ordeal. Many publications don't pay until after publication, which may take place several months or even more than a year after a piece is finished. Even after the article is published, payment may be held up for weeks, and telephone calls to complain go unanswered.

At the very least, low pay is a festering wound for freelancers, many of whom live in cramped apartments and can't afford health insurance. One might argue that these individuals should stop being "self-indulgent and undisciplined Bohemians" and land full-time jobs with the *Tribune* or a trade journal and "damn it, work hard like the rest of us Americans." But most media outlets behave like their corporate brethren. They have "downsized" or "rightsized" (fired or laid off full-time employees). They now "outsource" even more work to self-employed contractors who receive no fringe benefits.

Without a doubt, freelancing is here to stay, so the issue of poor pay needs to be addressed. Chronic underpayment diminishes not only the quality of writers' lives but the quality of journalism overall. As our essay on the *Tribune* relates, mature freelancers can't afford to continue writing for publications that reward their many hours of research, interviewing and writing with what amounts to minimum-wage scale.

The media are often criticized for an obsession with youth. Dictates from the advertising world are often blamed, but another reason is that only the young (or those with trust funds) can afford to play the reporting game. Freelancers for the *Sun-Times*, *The Reader* and the *Tribune* realize that, to pay the rent without mom and dad's help, they must move on to better-paying gigs. As they enter their 30s or 40s, they learn that writing for full-color, monthly magazines with perfumed inserts doesn't enable them to eke out more than a grainy, black-and-white existence. To support dependents or save for retirement — to become a responsible citizen, in other words, and perpetuate family values — often necessitates saying good-bye to journalism.

Not surprisingly, many freelancers drift toward better-paying careers in technical writing, public relations and marketing communications. Others may enroll in law school, go to Hollywood and write screenplays, or enter fields unrelated to communications. As our essay on *Advertising Age* indicates, getting paid by a corporate executive or a public relations firm to ghostwrite pays much better than writing under your own byline. It just doesn't *pay* to be a highly dedicated, full-time freelance journalist.

The damage is not merely to individuals but to society at large. Due to a lack of mature freelance journalists, the media is a shallower and murkier place in which to swim. The poverty many writers endure reflects, at the very least, ignorance in publishing and, more likely, a poverty of values among elite editors, publishers and media executives. The damage, however, extends well beyond the industry. The dearth of fairly compensated freelance journalists results in a diminished flow of thoughtful reporting, which a healthy democracy needs to inform and renew itself.

# Advertising Age

*By Anne Aldrich*

*Ad Age*, as it's known in the business, is a national weekly covering the advertising and marketing industries. By all accounts, writing for *Ad Age* is a great way to establish a name for yourself in the business and add impressive clips to your portfolio. Seasoned writers, however, may want to pass it up simply because of its low rates. As one writer put it, "Writing for *Ad Age* is fun but too time-intensive. The kind of investigative journalism pieces they require take too long to research and write."

The Chicago edition of *Ad Age* covers client and ad-agency activity for the Midwest market and features a weekly section devoted to a particular topic (*e.g.*, Hispanic marketing, newspapers, sales promotions). While much of the material is written by freelancers — on assignment — the Forum section accepts unsolicited essays.

Writers seeking assignments should know the coverage area and be able to stick to a narrowly defined assignment. "It's definitely for specialists who know Midwest agencies, issues and trends, and you should speak the lingo," says one regular contributor.

The time spent learning the coverage area and jargon can pay off in repeated assignments. "Once I proved myself and established a rapport with the editors, I consistently received assignments," affirmed a once-regular writer. "I could still be writing on a regular basis for them, but I gained enough experience and clips to move on to better-paying venues."

A benefit to becoming a "regular" is the opportunity to present unsolicited story ideas. "The editors I contacted always responded promptly to brief, insightful queries, and gave my story ideas careful consideration," said one favored writer.

Queries are responded to quickly (within a month). Once accepted, the article is usually published within six months. By all indications, the publication buys all rights and generally pays upon publication. No contracts are used, and the writers interviewed did not recall a clear kill-fee policy. Writers are not given galleys or consulted on the editing of their stories, but the editing tends to be light.

Rates vary widely. One writer indicated he was paid a dollar a word for a feature article and $200 for a brief Forum essay, while another said he was paid only $350 for a feature of more than 1,000 words. Evidently, negotiation is the key here. Expenses — such as telephone, fax and overnight-shipments — were promptly reimbursed.

A notable exception to the type of time-intensive, lower-paying articles characteristic of *Ad Age* is writing done for third parties — mostly public relations firms — and submitted to *Ad Age* to present a certain point of view on a product or client. In fact, several writers have "ghosted" articles on behalf of a third party and have been paid handsomely for their efforts — by the PR firm, not *Ad Age*. As with many trade magazines, it's easier to make a living by ghost-writing articles for private clients than it is to write directly for the publication itself.

Professional, courteous treatment is the rule at *Ad Age*. All writers interviewed were quick to point out how fairly they were dealt with, and how courteous the editors were, making it a pleasure to write for the publication.

# Chicago

*By Michael O'Neill*

*Chicago* magazine is a slick regional magazine whose aim is to feature the best of the Windy City. Typically covered are "Chicago's best-kept secrets," new restaurants, sports, politics, local celebrities, night life and other aspects of the greater Chicago area. A colorful, well-produced publication, *Chicago* has been accused of superficiality and yuppie values. These criticisms show, perhaps, in the magazine's emphasis on restaurants and profiles of Chicago professionals.

The magazine pays well, some say, but others suggest that the main reason that *Chicago's* rates aren't higher is that the magazine lacks competition. As the only major magazine of its kind in the area, *Chicago* can draw from a large pool of writers who have few alternatives for getting their regional features published.

Feature stories pay from $3,000 to $4,000, and department-length pieces from $1,000 to $1,500. Shorter pieces of about 250 words pay about a dollar a word. The kill fee is 25 percent, and no one we talked to had tried to renegotiate it. *Chicago* contracts claim First North American Serial rights, but some writers report having never signed a contract in all the time that they've written for the magazine.

Writers are paid generally right before the magazine comes out (each monthly issue is distributed at the end of the previous month), and expenses such as telephone, fax and delivery service are paid by the magazine as long as receipts are provided.

Some writers report having had pieces heavily rewritten, while others have had more positive experiences. Unsolicited manuscripts are rarely accepted. The best way to break in is to query an editor with your ideas, although more established writers telephone first to pitch an idea and follow up with a written proposal. As one writer said, "If you've got a story you can tailor to any section, you can get around an editor who isn't open to your idea."

While *Chicago* is interested in investigative journalism, it tends to run a number of puff pieces. The feeling of some of the writers we talked with was that it was fairly difficult to scope out what the magazine was looking for at any given time. There have been a number of changes in the editorial staff, and the turnover has created a certain amount of discord.

Inside information about the editors is not generally positive. Editor-in-chief Richard Babcock is widely disliked. Dan Santow is another editor that freelancers have had problems with, but he has since left the magazine.

Joanne Trestrail, *Chicago's* longtime managing editor, received high marks. So did senior editor Jan Parr, although one freelancer called her "unhelpful." Writers we spoke to praised these two editors for their skills in dealing with writers and in the editing of their pieces. Trestrail, however, quit *Chicago* in the spring of 1993 and took a job with the Books section of the *Chicago Tribune*.

Some writers spoke of reviewing galleys, whereas others weren't given the opportunity. Our advice is to request the right to see galleys once your assignment is accepted. If you make it clear in advance, you can avoid the unpleasant surprise of learning that your work has been extensively rewritten once it's on the newsstands.

All in all, it's best to know the editors' personalities since receptiveness to different ideas and the ability to work well with writers varies widely. Because of the many changes that the magazine has gone through, *Chicago* seems to be in a serious state of flux. Although one writer says some of the most gifted editors in the country are at *Chicago*, it's definitely a mixed bag. Proceed with caution.

# Chicago Reader

*By Sheila Malkind*

The *Chicago Reader* deals fairly with writers, according to interviews with three writers. One authored book reviews; another film reviews, Calendar and opinion pieces; the third, features and neighborhood news. In writing this piece, I am also drawing on my personal experience, since *The Reader* published a long feature of mine.

Business arrangements with *The Reader* are simple, straightforward and honest, although not financially rewarding for writers. Despite complaints that *The Reader* is "cheap," all agreed that payment is prompt — the first week of the month after a piece is published. Writers quoted rates of $80 for a film review; $100-$120 for Calendar, from $50 to $150 for Our Town, $225 for book reviews, $300 for Neighborhood News and $800 to $1,000 for features. Payment is rarely negotiable. There is no kill fee because there are almost no assignments.

Most articles are written on speculation, although writers may query editors first. The editors are known for being approachable. One writer said, "They'll talk to you beforehand about your idea, and might say, 'Gee, it doesn't make sense.'"

One writer advises, "Get a sense of the type of stories that fit within their *shtick* and send them some. They don't want stuff other papers are doing." Another writer said the philosophy seems to be, "If we like it, we'll run it; if we don't, we won't."

Writers should take note to be meticulous with research. There is a thorough and sometimes time-consuming process of copy-editing. The paper does not usually send galleys to writers for approval before press time.

One problem for freelancers is that it can take a long time for a piece to be published, depending on the backlog of stories on editors' desks. Stories may get bumped for months on end and, subsequently, payment gets bumped.

There is no contract between writer and *Reader*, but the writer does retain First North American Serial rights and can seek to publish the article elsewhere without consultation with *The Reader*.

*The Reader* can be summed up by one writer who called it, "Offbeat, open to new material but a little stingy."

# Chicago Sun-Times

By Aaron Cohen

The *Sun-Times* is a daily newspaper that tries hard to set itself apart from the competition. While the *Chicago Tribune* has a reputation for aiming at a more upscale suburban readership, the *Sun-Times* actively pursues an audience within the city limits. In addition to concentrating on local issues, the *Sun-Times* is priced lower than the *Tribune* and is published in a thick headline, tabloid format that's easy for CTA riders to notice and pick up every morning.

All of the respondents in our survey have expressed how, for a big-city daily, the *Sun-Times* is open and generally fair to freelancers. Persistence and fresh ideas are as important for writers here as anywhere else, and the editors usually have open ears. The pay is low but tends to be delivered promptly.

Arts and Show, Weekend Plus, Travel, and Home Life are the sections for which our respondents have written. Everyone said it's better to try—and often to retry—reaching editors by phone rather than by mail.

"Letters get thrown somewhere," one writer said. "The response is instant by phone. If you approach them with a good idea that's clear in your mind, make it a quick phone call. Make sure you sound like you have the necessary experience."

"Good ideas" for the Arts and weekend sections have to be the creative work of the writer. Don't expect an editor to provide the assignments. "They're looking for unpredictable, unconventional ideas," one writer said. "The Weekend Plus section is looking for offbeat types of stories, and you have to meet the unconventional ideas of editors. I've rarely been assigned anything."

Travel is not as offbeat as the Arts and Weekend sections, but the section tries to be lively. "They're looking for stuff that sets them apart from the *Tribune*," one writer explains. "They try to be sharper, faster, more interesting than the *Tribune*, with more of a city focus. Don't call up with 10 picnic-spot ideas in DuPage County."

Home Life looks for more serious topics, according to one writer. "The section looks for something of interest to homeowners and buyers. Read the section. They're interested in important issues or something helpful. They are not looking for puff pieces."

"Easy to work with" and "great" are words used to describe the editors. While there is a chain of command that could burden the process of assigning stories, the response to ideas is usually quick. The editors clearly explain their needs. Stories are edited for length, but no problems with rewrites have been reported.

Laura Emerick, Arts and Show editor, is described as "very busy" but not difficult. Weekend Editor Tim Bannon is "a little unconventional" and as approachable as Emerick. Steve Rynkiewicz is the Home Life editor.

Depending upon length of the story and number of sources used, the pay ranges from $100 to $200. On Sundays the paper runs "showbiz stories" that pay $50. Writers are generally paid at the end of the month or at the beginning of the month following publication. One writer said that "within five days of publication, there's a check in the mailbox."

Contracts are not used, and the general impression is that payment is nonnegotiable. Since the *Sun-Times* has such a local focus, one freelancer comments, "There's always a chance you can market a piece somewhere else outside their circulation." Another writer reports being able to resell a story to other newspapers.

A frustration of one freelancer is that *Sun-Times* staff writers "have first dibs on stories even if you make a proposal," which seems to be the case at many newspapers.

# Chicago Tribune

By Kurt Jacobsen

The *Chicago Tribune* is the city's highest circulation (and highest priced) daily paper. The good news is that, except for straight news features, *Tribune* editors are usually open to ideas. The trend, *Tribune* editors say, is toward increased use of freelance material, so there are plenty of opportunities here, especially in the Tempo, Arts and WomaNews sections.

The bad news is that the *Tribune* pays rather poorly, even if slightly better than rival *Sun-Times*. Contributors say the rates are "pretty low for a big-city newspaper," "pathetic" and "dreadful." When asked to consider the overall quality of the *Trib*, they say it falls "far short of its potential." A typical comment: "It's got enough resources to be a top-notch paper — like *The New York Times, Los Angeles Times* or *Washington Post* — but it isn't there yet." Still, it would be easy, says another contributor, "to write off the *Tribune* as stodgy and dull. The paper is trying to be more diverse and attentive to reporting local news."

Low pay aside, the editors treat writers reasonably well. "If you have a good feel for the section and the type of article they're looking for, they're a good outfit to work with." Getting in (and staying in) takes tenacity. Study the section and approach the editor when you have a suitable idea. "Be very organized when presenting an idea. If you are on target, they'll grab it," advises a writer. "Call Monday and Friday to reach editors," another writer suggests. "It's best to call first." Having a piece accepted does not mean it will be published, and you will not be paid until it is published. No one complained about censorship. Only once in a dozen interviews did a writer complain of having text butchered.

The key advantage that a freelancer reaps is obtaining *Trib* clips, which are important for opening doors to other publications. The poor pay, in the short run, might be acceptable. Few of the freelancers I contacted wrote for the *Trib* for more than a few years.

Relevant sections for freelancers are Tempo, The Arts on Friday and Sunday, WomaNews, the Overnight Page and Sunday magazine. Like most major papers, the *Trib* is bureaucratic. "The section editors don't always know what other sections are doing," a writer notes. Occasionally a writer loses work because his or her assignment may have also been assigned to someone writing for a different section. In one such instance, the Tempo editors gave the writer a 75 percent kill fee along with profuse apologies. No one mentions having been paid for expenses, but no one asked for expenses either.

Tempo and The Arts pay $250 to $350 for articles of 1,500-2,000 words. For pieces of 400-700 words, they pay $150. Tempo is about 30 percent freelance, but about half of its lead stories are written by freelancers. The Sunday magazine pays $500-$1,500, depending on length, and uses 50 percent to 75 percent freelance material. The paper has no official policy on kill fees. "We try to use everything we commission," a Tempo editor says. When a piece is killed, the fee is up to the editor.

It is, of course, the luck of the draw in hitting it off with editors. "The first editor and I just clicked," recalls one contributor. "The next editor didn't like anything I gave her." There were a number of complaints, even from veteran contributors, about slow responses to queries. Several writers attribute this to understaffing. The solution is to "keep pestering them." In general, writers find the *Tribune* edits their work with some care and, time permitting, consults the writer.

The *Tribune* runs about 15 book reviews (of a thousand words each) every week. There is a daily review in the Tempo section plus a Sunday Books pull-out section. The editors do not accept unsolicited reviews. If you have expertise in a given field, however, contact the editors and they will likely invite you to send a resume and sample book review.

In summary, the pay is low but getting *Tribune* clips is significant for novice freelancers. "I had a good experience except for the ridiculously low pay," one writer said. "I recommend it to people getting started."

# Crain's Chicago Business

*By Marilyn Soltis*

Described as "influential and newsy" by one writer, the publications at Crain's Communications — including *Advertising Age, Automotive News* and *Electronic Media* — are on top of the latest developments and trends in the business community. The demographics consist predominantly of highly educated males who want hands-on information unencumbered by technical jargon.

Be prepared if you want to pitch a story. Editors and staff are overworked and have no time to walk you through an assignment. Editors expect, and are accustomed to, a high degree of professionalism in their writers and are not interested in cultivating aspiring authors. The Take-Out section, the last remaining pages open to freelancers since the recession, is ruled by Lisa Keefe, editor for Special Sections, described as "not exactly a nurturing person."

The Options page is also open to freelancers. Glenn Coleman, Deputy Managing Editor, is described as very receptive to ideas and nice to work with. The Options page is a feature section focusing on interesting people and unusual places. But don't call on Thursdays because it's their busy day.

Unsolicited manuscripts are not welcomed and queries are unnecessary. Pick up the phone and call the editor. They are receptive to good ideas and can give an okay on a story as quickly as the same day in some circumstances. Stories are assigned two to four weeks in advance. Reports vary as to how clear and specific assignments are and how well the editors communicate with the writers. The use of contracts seems to be very casual. Some writers have a release form on file at *Crain's*, some have signed contracts that were not returned. Some writers said this was not a problem because of the specificity and timeliness of the articles.

Section editor Lisa Keefe tends to rewrite more than other editors. One writer advises examining the editorial calendar to Take-Out at least two months in advance and giving her specific ideas of a topic in that section while tying it to a specific Chicago corporation. An example would be to profile a corporation that is redoing its pension plans for human resource reasons and tying that into a local trend.

On the news side, *Crain's* is seeking scandal stories about Chicago executives breaking new ground or making major mistakes. The Take-Out section is looking for technological news that can be competitive. For the Benefits sections, *Crain's* is interested in stories such as how Chicago corporations are coping with the high cost of health care. Be specific and local in your choice of corporations.

Like many publications in the Chicago area, there is more glitter than gold in having a *Crain's* byline on your resume. Rates were reported at $11 to $12.50 per column inch. *Crain's* buys all rights and, if they can pick up your story and use it in their news service, they will not pay you again. Articles are generally so specific that they cannot be used again anyway. Kill fees are paid for unused stories. They pay expenses such as overnight delivery, fax, phone and mileage when necessary. Payment gets put into the system as soon as it has been edited and through the copy desk. It generally takes about three weeks and comes out the same week as the story.

Rewrites are common or virtually nonexistent, depending on the editor. Galleys are sometimes sent, but most changes are discussed over the phone.

The benefits of writing for *Crain's* reach beyond payment. While the compensation is not particularly competitive for the amount of work and research put into an article, the byline is highly respected and garners local attention. Other Chicago-based magazine editors will be familiar with your work. One writer reported that he received more attention from a Take-Out story than he did for a longer feature in a national business magazine.

To sum it up, *Crain's* is a good vehicle for professional journalists to use for name recognition and as a springboard to other business and local publications. It is not a place where the more inexperienced writer can learn the ropes or be cultivated by nurturing editors.

# In These Times

*By Steve Askin*

Can a financially troubled magazine that alienated many of its freelance writers by failing to pay them, redeem its reputation and again become a good outlet for those whose work challenges the political status quo?

That's the big question facing *In These Times (ITT)*. We don't have a firm answer yet, but there is reason to hope that the Chicago-based "alternative newsmagazine" is ready to mend its once-irresponsible ways.

After years of often-bitter conflict with writers, *ITT* has reached an agreement with the National Writers Union to provide $75,000 to pay off its back debts to freelance writers. If successfully implemented, the pact will make *ITT* the first Chicago-area publication to accept the NWU Standard Journalism Contract, thereby pushing it to the forefront among area publications on such key issues as prompt payment on acceptance, abolition of kill fees and protection against unauthorized electronic resale of writers' copy. The agreement with *ITT* was still tentative when *BYLINE* went to press. NWU members would therefore be well advised to check with the union before writing for *ITT*, and all writers should proceed with caution based on knowledge of the paper's past record.

**Conflict-Ridden History**

Founded in 1975 as an independent socialist newsweekly, *ITT* long ago won a reputation as a great outlet for groundbreaking stories other publications wouldn't touch. "It has an intelligent readership, is very lightly edited, and it can be a lot of fun to write for because it gives you the freedom and flexibility to say what you want to say," says Daniel Lazare, a widely-published New York writer on economic affairs.

But, as the magazine limped from one financial crisis to another, it infuriated many writers. The problem was not just that *ITT* failed to pay its debts but, worse yet, according to many writers, the publication failed to warn them in advance about the near certainty that payment would be delayed.

"I understand the financial pressures such magazines face," says Brett Campbell, a former editor of another small opinion journal, *The Texas Observer.* But what he found intolerable, Campbell said in a letter to *ITT*, is "[your] assigning stories, promising payment, accepting them and running them in your paper all without telling eager writers that you knew there was little chance of them being paid on time as promised, if ever."

For many years, the NWU fought on a case-by-case basis to win payment for aggrieved writers. In the late 1980s, *ITT* signed a contract with the NWU, becoming the first Chicago-area publication to do so. That contract made it possible for the union ultimately to assure payment for writers who used our grievance process. In 1991 through 1993, the NWU won more than $50,000 in back pay for more than 50 *ITT* contributors. But hundreds of other writers, especially those who were not union members, failed to exercise their grievance-process rights and never got paid.

As new grievances kept flowing to the union, the NWU stepped up the pressure for systematic reform.

**Signs of Change**
Last year, under pressure from the union, *ITT* launched a major fund-raising effort to settle all back debts not just to writers but to printers, mailing houses and even the Internal Revenue Service. While that drive was under way, the NWU found a temporary solution that stopped the flood of grievances: *ITT* editors agreed temporarily to warn all writers in advance that they might never be paid, and to ask them to write for the magazine only if willing to donate their labor.

In January 1994, after *ITT* raised close to $350,000 through its refinance effort, NWU and *ITT* negotiated a tentative agreement on a plan to settle back debts and guarantee full protection for the rights of all future freelance contributors. That agreement, which was still awaiting approval by the union's *ITT* bargaining unit when this book went to press, would establish a $75,000 fund to settle all past freelance debts. Writers and photographers would be given until mid-May to submit payment claims; if the valid claims exceeded $75,000, the money would be divided among freelance creditors in proportion to the amount owed.
For future freelance contributors, the agreement's most important provisions are those that guarantee NWU members and only NWU members the right to use the Standard Journalism Contract. That contract, which provides the strongest protections for freelance writers available in the publishing industry, provides that:
- All writers be paid within 30 days after submission of a contracted story, and agreed-upon expenses be reimbursed within 15 days after submission.
- There is no kill fee: contracted work that meets the terms of the assignment is paid for whether published or not.
- All rights except for one-time North American print publication rights remain the property of the writer.
- The writer has the right to take disputes about payments or other matters to an independent arbitrator.

*ITT* further agreed to provide extra protection against payment delays. NWU members who use the union contract will be entitled to ask for steep interest payments if the paper fails to pay on time.

In addition, *ITT* will limit its past practice of requesting that many writers contribute their work "on spec." *ITT* may no longer request "on spec" submissions from NWU members who have been published at least twice in the magazine and elect to use the union contract.

In return, the union agreed to one major concession: it abandoned any attempt to control *ITT* pay rates. Under the old contract, *ITT* was required to pay a minimum of 16 cents per word for stories, and $65 each for photographs. In the future, each writer or photographer will need to negotiate his or her rate individually. Union negotiators made this concession only after carefully examining records submitted to the union by *ITT*. Because those records document a large and consistent operating deficit, and because *ITT* writers have repeatedly said that fair treatment and not high payment is their main goal, the union reluctantly agreed to give up the negotiated rate.

**The Bottom Line**

*ITT*'s financial future remains uncertain in an era when many small, left-leaning periodicals (among them *The Guardian* of New York and the liberal religious weekly *Christianity and Crisis*), have been forced out of business by lack of funds. But the new agreement with the NWU provides new hope that writers will be treated fairly... and that this leading outlet for political and cultural dissent will flourish again.

Writers who expect to be paid for their work should approach *ITT* with caution. They must negotiate payment rates in advance since *ITT* no longer has a standard rate. Union writers would be well-advised to request not less than the old contract rate (16 cents per word) but should not be surprised if the magazine insists on paying less.

*ITT* has experience helping writers obtain special grants for ground-breaking (and time-consuming) investigative projects. If you have a strong investigative track record on issues of interest to *ITT*, consider asking if the magazine could help you raise funds to research and write such articles.

NWU members must specifically request the Standard Journalism Contract since the union can do nothing to protect them unless they have done so. Given the magazine's past track record, It would be the height of folly to write for *ITT* without such protection. For the same reason, nonmembers who are considering writing for *ITT* would be well-advised to join the NWU since the union contract offers the best protection against future problems.

# By THE BACK

## What Writers Need To Know About the NWU

# A Better Contract

## Improving the Treatment of Freelance Writers: A Statement from the National Writers Union

Magazine publishers continue buying and selling properties, restructuring their ad rates and reshuffling editorial priorities. But one thing remains depressingly constant: the deterioration of fees, working conditions and contracts for freelance writers, without whose work few publications could survive.

The National Writers Union believes it is past time for publishers of periodicals to reverse this trend and conform with practices considered reasonable in other businesses. Fair and professional standards for freelancers can only enhance the quality of periodicals and help stabilize the industry.

The NWU Journalism Campaign suggests members use its Standard Journalism Contract, which is a simple, one-page document. The contract is the centerpiece of a movement to improve working conditions, correct the balance of power and raise professional standards in the periodicals industry.

The Standard Contract is a benchmark against which to measure other contracts, a vehicle for teaching editors to treat writers with respect and a rallying point for journalists. Above all, it's a practical instrument for writers to get better terms every time they negotiate an assignment.

Developed by full-time freelancers, the contract outlines a healthy, achievable relationship between writer and publisher. Written in clear, non-technical language, it accounts for the concerns of both writers and publishers, specifies mutual responsibilities and respects the realities of the writing process.

Copies of the contract are available only to NWU members, who first must attend a training session on how to use the contract and how to negotiate more skillfully. Thus, the actual text of the contract is not reproduced in this volume. The principles embodied in the contract, however, are described below.

### 1. One Fee, One Use

For decades, magazines bought first North American Serial rights only, which allowed them to publish the piece once. If they wanted to resell or reprint, they had to get the writer's permission and negotiate a fee.

Increasingly, writers are required to sign off on a long list of other rights — including syndication, anthology, foreign reprints and electronic database — that the publisher seizes for no extra fee. Some magazines require that writers sign "work-for-hire" contracts, handing over the copyright to the publishing company, which can use the piece as it pleases.

While we do not oppose a writer's selling additional rights, we do condemn publishers' theft of these rights. Magazines already pay too little for one-time publication. If they can resell our work over and over, their profits increase while our rates effectively plummet.

## 2. Full Payment on Submission of Contracted Work

This principle encompasses three issues: precise contracts, timely payment and the use of "kill fees." A writer who fulfills the terms of an assignment should be paid immediately and in full.

Occasionally a piece is killed because the writer has failed to fulfill the assignment. But we've experienced the dramatic increase in the capricious use of the kill fee. Many magazines overassign, expecting to kill as many as two or three pieces. Assuming little financial risk, editors freely change their minds or decide not to put time into a rewrite. With full inventories, they may take months to read a piece submitted on deadline — and meanwhile, the writer waits for the fee.

Editors must assign judiciously, write careful assignment letters in consultation with the writer, then pay in full — *not* on publication, *not* on acceptance but when the work is done. An editor who is unhappy with the job has the option not to work with the writer again.

## 3. Fair Rates

Our writers contribute to a wide spectrum of publications, from local newspapers to corporate newsletters to national magazines, and their rates vary accordingly. While we can't set a universal fair rate, we can almost categorically say that what journalists are paid is unfair. In real dollars, rates have gone down in the past decades. Magazines establish ceilings that even long-term contributors can't break through. There is scarcely a freelance journalist — seasoned, "successful" ones included — who makes more than $25,000 a year, and that's without benefits, unemployment insurance or Social Security contributions.

## 4. Arbitration

Disputes between publishers and writers usually can be handled through the grievance process of the National Writers Union. But if an impasse is reached and the only option is to go to court, most writers lose by default: they simply can't afford the money or the time. An arbitration clause enables writers to defend their rights without financial burden and encourages publishers to honor their contracts.

*For more information about the Journalism Campaign, please write to NWU Chicago, P.O. Box 2537, Chicago, IL 60690-2537; or leave a message after dialing (312) 348-1300.*

# Byline Contributors

The following is a list of NWU volunteers who graciously offered their time and skills to complete this book.

**Anne Aldrich** runs a Chicago-based creative services firm specializing in direct marketing and advertising.

**Steve Askin** is the National Writers Union's *In These Times* Grievance officer since mid-1992 and a former *ITT* Africa correspondent. He freelanced for the paper for more than a decade, starting in the late 1970s.

**Jeff Black** is an Evanston-based freelance writer. Besides corporate and educational projects, he has written for a variety of publications and is the author of two novels.

**Aaron Cohen** is a Chicago-area freelance writer. He has written about literature, music and legal issues for a small number of publications across North America.

**Judith Cooper**, Internal Vice President of the NWU, is a fiction writer who support herself by writing industrial scripts.

**R. H. Crane** has written a book of poetry, art and geometry, *Crossed Silver,* published by Milne, McKinnon & Christie.

**Jerry DeMuth**, *Byline* co-chair, writes regularly on business, finance and real estate and occasionally on arts and entertainment for consumer and trade publications. He has been freelancing full-time since 1979.

**Ron Dorfman** has been a newspaper and magazine editor in Chicago for the past 30 years. He is currently Director of Publications for the Field Museum.

**Steve Eckardt** is a Chicago-based freelance writer who has written on travel and politics, among other topics.

**Bill Granger**, a novelist whose last book was *Burning the Apostle,* freelances a regular essay for the *Chicago Tribune Sunday Magazine.* When he was a writer for the *Chicago Sun-Times,* he was a unit vice-chairman of the American Newspaper Guild there.

**Martha Hyzer**, *Byline* survey director, is a Chicago-area freelance writer.

**Kurt Jacobsen** is a Chicago-area freelance writer.

**LeVaughn Jones** is an information specialist whose company, Knowledge Tree, provides library and online database research services to individuals and small businesses.

**Michele Kelly**, *Byline* co-chair, is founder of LoDestro Public Relations in Chicago's west suburbs. She writes news articles, marketing collateral and mystery novels.

**Joen Kinnan** is a freelance writer who specializes in medical, pharmaceutical writing and desktop publishing.

**Sheila Malkind** is a freelance writer and photographer.

**Dave McCracken** is a Chicago-area writer and editor.

**Gary Melhart** is a freelance writer specializing in telecommunications.

**Deborah Miller** is a training and documentation consultant specializing in computer software.

**Susan Nelson** is a Chicago-area freelance writer and editor.

**Mike O'Neill** is a Chicago-based freelance writer, editor and translator, fluent in French and Russian.

**Nance Seiple**, a consultant and writer involved in medical communications, specializes in continuing education programs for health-care professionals. She also trains sales representatives for medical devices and pharmaceutical companies.

**Betty Sherwood** is a Chicago-area writer. Her company, Second Wave Computing, Inc., specializes in computer writing and desktop design.

**Marilyn Soltis** is a freelance journalist/writer whose work covers an eclectic variety of subjects in the fields of medicine, law, business, entertainment, food and travel.

**Pam Sourelis** is a fiction writer, editor and writing instructor.

**Len Strazewski** is a veteran freelance writer specializing in business and technology topics. He also writes comic books.

**Alice Sunshine** is a regional organizer for the NWU and a freelance journalist.

**Sue Telingator**, *Byline* co-chair, is a Chicago-area ghostwriter and journalist whose first book, *The Chicago Arts Guide*, was published in 1993 by Chicago Review Press.

**John Vikiras** is a Chicago-area short story fiction writer.

**Keith Watson**, NWU Chicago chair and former journalist, is a freelance writer specializing in corporate communications.

**Kathy Wilson** is a journalist who has worked for *The New York Times*.

**S.L. Wisenberg** is the founder of Red Fish Writing Workshop and has written features, essays and reportage for *The Miami Herald, Chicago Tribune, Chicago Sun-Times, Crain's Chicago Business, The Reader, Wigwag, In These Times* and other publications.

**K.J. Zarker** is a Chicago-based freelance writer and journalist who has written for art publications, academic publications and other media.

# Writer's Bloc

## Founded in 1981, the NWU Knows that Good Writing Must Be Organized

Too often in negotiations with publishers, words fail. Not for lack of eloquence but for lack of power. Few writers acting alone have the clout to confront powerful publishers and win justice. That's why, in 1981, writers began organizing the National Writers Union. The NWU blends old-fashioned union idealism with some of the newest innovations in worker protection.

In case after case, the NWU has fought institutionalized abuse of writers: late or denied payments, arbitrary and capricious use of kill fees, and practices ranging from enforced work-for-hire to outright theft. American and European unions have marveled at the NWU grievance process, which has recovered three quarters of a million dollars for writers. Other unions study the NWU to learn the latest ways to organize people who work independently.

**Membership Qualifications:**
A writer is eligible if he or she has published a book, a play, three articles, five poems, a short story, or an equivalent amount of newsletter, publicity, technical, commercial, government or institutional copy. A writer is also eligible if he or she has written an equal amount of unpublished material and is actively writing and attempting to have work published. Dues, based on annual writing income, are low for a union or professional association.

**A Community of Writers:**
NWU members range from best-selling novelists to beginning magazine writers. The NWU welcomes all writers: writers of color, gay and lesbian writers, and writers of all political stripes. In addition to offering journalists a variety of services described in detail in this volume, the NWU serves the following:

■ *Book Authors:*
The NWU Book Campaign has waged a campaign to pressure the publishing industry to halt its worst practices. In the process, the NWU has recovered hundreds of thousands of dollars in lost payments for authors. The NWU is not afraid to make waves and take on publishers big and small. The union picketed multinational Penguin USA after the company refused to agree to minimum terms. The NWU also confronted Simon & Schuster for depriving a union writer of hundreds of thousands of dollars in royalties. In addition to handling grievances, the NWU offers up-to-date information on agents and advice about negotiating better contracts.

■ *Technical Writers:*
While technical writers are often relatively well paid, they need protection as well. For years, profiteering agents have taken fees as high as 40 percent. That's why the NWU created the Technical Writers Hotline in San Francisco. It's the best, fairest source of freelance contract work for union technical writers.

■ *From Poets ... to Practical Writers:*
The NWU represents all independent writers, whether they work in fiction and poetry, or write public relations pieces for industry, government or non-profit organizations. All members receive the same grievance handling and benefits regardless of income level.

Support for All Writers: The NWU organized street demonstrations in support of Salman Rushdie, opposed prurient restrictions on grants from the National Endowment for the Arts, and marched against restrictive taxation on artists and writers. In 1992, the NWU organized dozens of writers' groups across the nation for Writers' Rights Day, which has become an annual event. The NWU has also begun an Electronic Rights Project to monitor the growing use and abuse of copyright in computerized data bases—a matter of vital importance to writers now ... and in the future.

National and Local Activism: The NWU has more than 10 regional units operating across the nation. Local meetings—in Chicago, New York, Boston, San Francisco and several other cities—help writers combat isolation and exchange practical information. Local units sponsor meetings with editors and agents, conferences and events from multicultural readings to observances of Writers' Rights Day. NWU national and local campaigns produce results because members make calls, hold meetings and stuff envelopes—whatever it takes to get the message across. That's why, in less than 15 years, the NWU has succeeded where others have failed. According to *The New York Times,* the NWU is one of the nation's two most important writers' organizations.

Union Democracy: The NWU sets the standard for union democracy. All leadership is directly elected by the membership, and records and meetings are open to all. The NWU is affiliated with the United Auto Workers and has stood side by side with other unions. No one is barred from membership in the NWU or shall be in any way discriminated against on the basis of race, age, sex, sexual orientation, disability, national origin, religion or ideology.

It's Time to Join: Just fill in the information below and send to NWU Chicago, P.O. Box 2537, Chicago, IL 60690-2537. Or call (312) 348-1300 and request that a complete application be sent to your address.

Name

Street Address

City					State			Zip Code

Telephone

249006